CAMBRIDGE LIBRARY COLLECTION

Books of enduring scholarly value

Philosophy

This series contains both philosophical texts and critical essays about philosophy, concentrating especially on works originally published in the eighteenth and nineteenth centuries. It covers a broad range of topics including ethics, logic, metaphysics, aesthetics, utilitarianism, positivism, scientific method and political thought. It also includes biographies and accounts of the history of philosophy, as well as collections of papers by leading figures. In addition to this series, primary texts by ancient philosophers, and works with particular relevance to philosophy of science, politics or theology, may be found elsewhere in the Cambridge Library Collection.

A Defence of Usury

The utilitarian philosopher and jurist Jeremy Bentham (1748–1832) argues in this collection of letters for the cessation of government control of the rate of interest. The work first appeared in 1787 and is reissued here in the version published in Dublin in 1788. The final letter, addressed to Adam Smith, is a response to Smith's *Wealth of Nations* (1776), arguing against the limits to inventive industry forced by the restriction on rates. Throughout the work is Bentham's emphasis on the value, both ethical and practical, of allowing private citizens to regulate their own financial dealings. Bentham offers a sophisticated philosophical, economic and political analysis of 'usury' and in so doing provides a template for a wider liberal view. Influential at the time of publication, the work still retains its significance in making a case for the proper relationship between the individual and the state.

Cambridge University Press has long been a pioneer in the reissuing of out-of-print titles from its own backlist, producing digital reprints of books that are still sought after by scholars and students but could not be reprinted economically using traditional technology. The Cambridge Library Collection extends this activity to a wider range of books which are still of importance to researchers and professionals, either for the source material they contain, or as landmarks in the history of their academic discipline.

Drawing from the world-renowned collections in the Cambridge University Library and other partner libraries, and guided by the advice of experts in each subject area, Cambridge University Press is using state-of-the-art scanning machines in its own Printing House to capture the content of each book selected for inclusion. The files are processed to give a consistently clear, crisp image, and the books finished to the high quality standard for which the Press is recognised around the world. The latest print-on-demand technology ensures that the books will remain available indefinitely, and that orders for single or multiple copies can quickly be supplied.

The Cambridge Library Collection brings back to life books of enduring scholarly value (including out-of-copyright works originally issued by other publishers) across a wide range of disciplines in the humanities and social sciences and in science and technology.

A Defence of Usury

*Shewing the Impolicy of the Present Legal Restraints
on the Terms of Pecuniary Bargains,
in a Series of Letters to a Friend*

JEREMY BENTHAM

University Printing House, Cambridge, CB2 8BS, United Kingdom

Published in the United States of America by Cambridge University Press, New York

Cambridge University Press is part of the University of Cambridge.
It furthers the University's mission by disseminating knowledge in the pursuit of
education, learning and research at the highest international levels of excellence.

www.cambridge.org
Information on this title: www.cambridge.org/9781108066945

© in this compilation Cambridge University Press 2014

This edition first published 1788
This digitally printed version 2014

ISBN 978-1-108-06694-5 Paperback

A

DEFENCE

OF

USURY.

DEFENCE of USURY;

Shewing the Impolicy of the

PRESENT LEGAL RESTRAINTS

ON THE TERMS OF

PECUNIARY BARGAINS

IN A

SERIES OF LETTERS TO A FRIEND.

TO WHICH IS ADDED,

A LETTER

TO

ADAM SMITH, Esq; LL, D.

On the Discouragements opposed by the above

Restraints to the Progress of

INVENTIVE INDUSTRY.

BY

JEREMY BENTHAM, of Lincoln's Inn, Esq.

DUBLIN:

Printed for Messrs. D. WILLIAMS, COLLES, WHITE, BYRNE, LEWIS, JONES, and MOORE.

MDCCLXXXVIII.

CONTENTS.

LET-

CONTENTS.

LETTER IV.

LETTER V.

LETTER VI.

LETTER VII.

LET-

CONTENTS.

LET-

CONTENTS.

LETTER XIII.

DEFENCE

A DEFENCE

OF

U S U R Y.

LETTER I.

Introduction.

Crichoff, in White Ruſſia,

January 1787.

A MONG the various ſpecies or modifications of liberty, of which on different occaſions we have heard ſo much in England, I do not recollect ever ſeeing any thing yet offered in

behalf

behalf of the *liberty of making one's own terms in money bargains.* From fo general and univerfal a neglect, it is an old notion of mine, as you well know, that this meek and unaffuming fpecies of liberty has been fuffering much injuftice.

A fancy has taken me, juft now, to trouble you with my reafons : which, if you think them capable of anfwer-ing any good purpofe, you may for-ward to the prefs : or in the other cafe, what will give you lefs trouble, to the fire.

In a word, the propofition I have been accuftomed to lay down to my-felf on this fubject is the following one,

one, viz. that *no man of ripe years and of found mind, acting freely, and with his eyes open, ought to be hindered, with a view to his advantage, from making fuch bargain, in the way of obtaining money, as he thinks fit ; nor,* (what is a neceffary confequence) *any body hindered from fupplying him, upon any terms he thinks proper to accede to.*

This propofition, were it to be received, would level, you fee, at one ftroke, all the barriers which law, either ftatute or common, have in their united wifdom fet up, either againft the crying fin of Ufury, or againft the hard-named and little-heard-of practice of Champerty ; to which we muft alfo add a portion of the multifarious, and

as

as little heard-of offence, of Maintenance.

On this occafion, were it any individual antagonift I had to deal with,
my part would be a fmooth and eafy
one. " You, who fetter contracts ;
" you, who lay reftraints on the li-
" berty of man, it is for you" (I
fhould fay) " to affign a reafon for your
" doing fo." That contracts in general ought to be obferved, is a rule, the
propriety of which, no man was ever
yet found wrong-headed enough to
deny ; if this cafe is one of the excep-
tions (for fome doubtlefs there are)
which the fafety and welfare of every
fociety require fhould be taken out of
that general rule, in this cafe, as in all
thofe

thofe others, it lies upon him, who al-
ledges the neceffity of the exception, to
produce a reafon for it.

This, I fay, would be a fhort and
very eafy method with an individual :
but as the world has no mouth of its
own to plead by, no certain attorney
by which it can " come and defend
" this force and injury," I muft even
find arguments for it at a venture,
and ranfack my own imagination for
fuch phantoms as I can find to fight
with.

In favour of the reftraints oppofed
to the fpecies of liberty I contend for,
I can imagine but five arguments.

1. Pre-

1. Prevention of ufury.

2. Prevention of prod'gality.

3. Protection of indigence againft extortion.

4. Repreffion of the temerity of pro-jectors.

5. Protection of fimplicity againft impofition.

Of all thefe in their order,

LETTER

L E T T E R II.

Reafons for Reftraint.—Prevention of Ufury.

I Will begin with the *prevention* of *ufury :* becaufe in the found of the word *ufury* lies, I take it, the main ftrength of the argument : or, to fpeak ftrictly, of what is of more importance than all argument, of the hold which the opinion I am combating has obtained on the imaginations and paffions of mankind.

Ufury

Ufury is a bad thing, and as fuch ought to be prevented : ufurers are a bad fort of men, a very bad fort of men, and as fuch ought to be punifh-ed and fuppreffed. Thefe are among the ftring of propofitions which every man finds handed down to him from his progenitors : which moft men are difpofed to accede to without examina-tion, and indeed not unnaturally nor even unreafonably difpofed, for it is impoffible the bulk of mankind fhould find leifure, had they the abi-lity, to examine into the grounds of an hundredth part of the rules and maxims, which they find themfelves obliged to act upon. Very good apo-logy this for John Trot : but a little

more

more inquifitivenefs may be required of legiflators.

You, my friend, by whom the true force of words is fo well underftood, have, I am fure, gone before me in perceiving, that to fay ufury is a thing to be prevented, is neither more or lefs than begging the matter in queftion. I know of but two definitions that can poffibly be given of ufury ; one is, the taking of a greater intereft than the law allows of : this may be ftiled the *political* or *legal* definition. The other is the taking of a greater intereft than it is ufual for men to give and take : this may be ftiled the *moral* one : and this, where the law has not interfered, is plainly enough the only one. It is plain, that in order for ufury to be prohibited by law, a pofitive defcription muft have been found for it by law, fixing, or rather fuperfeding, the moral one. To fay then that ufury is a thing that ought to be prevented, is faying neither more nor lefs, than that the utmoft rate of intereft which fhall be taken ought to be fixed ; and that fixation enforced by penalties, or fuch other means, if any, as may anfwer the purpofe of preventing the breach of it. A law punifhing ufury fuppofes, therefore, a law fixing the allowed legal rate of intereft : and the propriety of the penal law muft depend upon the propriety of the fimply-prohibitive

hibitive, or, if you pleafe, declaratory one.

One thing then is plain ; that, antecedently to cuftom growing from convention, there can be no fuch thing as ufury : for what rate of intereft is there that can naturally be more proper than another ? what natural fixed price can there be for the ufe of money more than for the ufe of any other thing ? Were it not then for cuftom, ufury, confidered in a moral view, would not then fo much as admit of a definition : fo far from having exiftence, it would not fo much as be conceivable : nor therefore could the law, in the definition it took upon itfelf to

give

give of fuch offence, have fo much as
a guide to fteer by. Cuftom therefore is the fole bafis, which, either the
moralift in his rules and precepts, or
the legiflature in his injunctions, can
have to build upon. But what bafis
can be more weak or unwarrantable,
as a ground for coercive meafures,
than cuftom refulting from free
choice ? My neighbours, being at liberty, have happened to concur among
themfelves in dealing at a certain rate
of intereft. I, who have money to
lend, and Titius, who wants to borrow
it of me, would be glad, the one of us
to accept, the other to give, an intereft
fomewhat higher than theirs : why is
the liberty they exercife to be made a
                                    pre-

pretence for depriving me and Titius of ours ?

Nor has blind cuftom, thus made the fole and arbitrary guide, any thing of fteadinefs or uniformity in its deci-fions : it has varied, from age to age, in the fame country : it varies, from country to country, in the fame age : and the legal rate has varied along with it : and indeed, with regard to times paft, it is from the legal rate, more rea-dily than from any other fource, that we collect the cuftomary. Among the Romans, till the time of Juftinian, we find it as high as 12 per cent. : in Eng-land, fo late as the time of Henry VIII. we find it at 10 per cent. : fucceeding

ftatutes

ftatutes reduced, it to 8, then to 6, and laftly to 5, where it ftands at prefent. Even at prefent in Ireland it is at 6 per cent. ; and in the Weft Indies at 8 per cent. ; and in Hindoftan, where there is no rate limited by law, the loweft cuftomary rate is 10 or 12. At Conftantinople, in certain cafes, as I have been well informed, thirty per cent. is a common rate. Now, of all thefe widely different rates, what one is there that is intrinfically more proper than another ? What is it that evidences this propriety in each inftance ? what but the mutual convenience of the parties, as manifefted by their confent ? It is convenience then that has produced whatever there has been of cuftom in the matter :

matter : What can there then be in cuftom, to make it a better guide than the
convenience which gave it birth ? and
what is there in convenience, that
fhould make it a worfe guide in one
cafe than in another ? It would be
convenient to me to give 6 per cent.
for money : I wifh to do fo. " No,"
(fays the law) " you fhan't."—Why
fo ? " Becaufe it is not convenient to
your neighbour to give above 5 for it."
Can any thing be more abfurd than fuch
a reafon ?

Much has not been done, I think,
by legiflators as yet in the way of fixing the price of other commodities :
and, in what little has been done, the
probity of the intention has, I believe,

in

in general, been rather more unquef-
tionable than the rectitude of the principle, or the felicity of the refult.   Putting money out at intereft, is exchang-
ing prefent money for future : but why
a policy, which, as applied to ex-
changes in general, would be generally
deemed abfurd and mifchievous, fhould
be deemed neceffary in the inftance of
this particular kind of exchange, mankind are as yet to learn.   For him who
takes as much as he can get for the ufe
of any other fort of thing, an houfe for
inftance, there is no particular appellation, nor any mark of difrepute : nobody is afhamed of doing fo, nor is it
ufual fo much as to profefs to do otherwife.   Why a man who takes as much
as he can get, be it fix, or feven, or
eight,

eight, or ten per cent. for the ufe of
a fum of money fhould be called ufurer, fhould be loaded with an oppro-
brious name, any more than if he had
bought a houfe with it, and made a
proportionable profit by the houfe, is
more than I can fee.

Another thing I would alfo wifh to
learn, is, why the legiflator fhould be
more anxious to limit the rate of intereft one way, than the other ? why he
fhould fet his face againft the owners
of that fpecies of property more than of
any other ? why he fhould make it his
bufinefs to prevent their getting *more*
than a certain price for the ufe of it, rather than to prevent their getting *lefs ?*
why, in fhort, he fhould not take means
for

for making it penal to offer lefs, for example, than 5 per cent. as well as to accept more? Let any one that can, find
an anfwer to thefe queftions ; it is more
than I can do : I except always the diftant and imperceptible advantage, of
finking the price of goods of all kinds;
and, in that remote way, multiplying
the future enjoyment of individuals.
But this was a confideration by far too
diftant and refined, to have been the
original ground for confining the limitation to this fide.

LETTER

L E T T E R III.

Reasons for Restraint.—Prevention of Prodigality.

HAVING done with sounds, I come gladly to propositions; which, as far as they are true in point of fact, may deserve the name of reasons. And first, as to the efficacy of such restrictive laws with regard to the *prevention of prodigality.*

That

That prodigality is a bad thing, and that the prevention of it is a proper object for the legiſlator to propoſe to himſelf, ſo long as he confines himſelf to, what I look upon as, proper meaſures, I have no objection to allow, at leaſt for the purpoſe of the argument ; though, were this the principal queſtion, I ſhould look upon it as incumbent on me to place in a fair light the reaſons there may be for doubting, how far, with regard to a perſon arrived at the age of diſcretion, third perſons may be competent judges, which of two pains may be of greater force and value to him, the preſent pain of reſtraining his preſent defires, or the future contingent pain he may be ex
poſed

pofed to fuffer from the want to which
the expence of gratifying thefe defires
may hereafter have reduced him. To
prevent our doing mifchief to one another, it is but too neceffary to put
bridles into all our mouths : it is neceffary to the tranquillity and very being of fociety : but that the tacking
of leading-ftrings upon the backs of
grown perfons, in order to prevent
their doing themfelves a mifchief, is
not neceffary either to the being or
tranquillity of fociety, however conducive to its well-being, I think cannot
be difputed. Such paternal, or, if you
pleafe, maternal care, may be a good
work, but it certainly is but a work of
fupererogation.

For

For my own part, I muſt confeſs, that ſo long as ſuch methods only are employed as to me appear proper ones; and ſuch there are, I ſhould not feel myſelf diſinclined to ſee ſome meaſures taken for the reſtraining of prodigality: but this I can not look upon as being of the number. My reaſons I will now endeavour to lay be- fore you.

In the firſt place, I take it, that it is neither natural nor uſual for prodigals, as ſuch, to betake themſelves to this method, I mean, that of giving a rate of intereſt above the ordinary one, to ſupply their wants.

In

In the firſt place, no man, I hope
you will allow, prodigal or not prodigal, ever thinks of borrowing money to
ſpend, ſo long as he has ready money
of his own, or effects which he can
turn into ready money without loſs.
And this deduction ſtrikes off what, I
ſuppoſe, you will look upon as the
greateſt proportion of the perſons ſubject, at any given time, to the imputation of prodigality.

In the next place, no man, in ſuch
a country as Great Britain at leaſt, has
occaſion, nor is at all likely, to take
up money at an extraordinary rate of
intereſt, who has ſecurity to give, equal
to that upon which money is commonly

ly to be had at the higheſt ordinary
rate. While ſo many advertiſe, as are
to be ſeen every day advertiſing, money
to be lent at five per cent. what ſhould
poſſeſs a man, who has any thing to
offer that can be called a ſecurity, to
give, for example, ſix per cent. is more
than I can conceive.

You may ſay, perhaps, that a man
who wiſhes to lend his money out upon ſecurity, wiſhes to have his intereſt
punctually, and that without the expence, and hazard, and trouble, and
odium of going to law ; and that, on
this account, it is better to have a ſober man to deal with than a prodigal.
So far I allow you ; but were you to
add,

add, that on this account it would be neceſſary for a prodigal to offer more than another man, there I ſhould diſagree with you. In the firſt place, it is not ſo eaſy a thing, nor, I take it, a common thing, for the lender upon ſecurity to be able to judge, or even to form any attempt to judge, whether the conduct of one who offers to borrow his money is, or is not of ſuch a caſt, as to bring him under this deſcription. The queſtion, prodigal or not prodigal, depends upon two pieces of information ; neither of which, in general, is very eaſy to come at : on the one hand, the amount of his means and reaſonable expectations ; on the other hand, the amount of his ex-

C   penditure.

penditure. The goodnefs or badnefs of the fecurity is a queftion of a very different nature : upon this head, every man has a known and ready means of obtaining that fort of information, which is the moft fatisfactory the nature of things affords, by going to his lawyer. It is accordingly, I take it, on their lawyers opinion, that lenders in general found their determination in thefe cafes, and not upon any calculations they may have formed, concerning the receipt and expenditure of the borrower. But even fuppofing a man's difpofition to prodigality to be ever fo well known, I take it there are always enough to be found, to whom fuch a difpofition would be rather an inducement than an objection, fo long

as

as they were fatisfied with the fecurity.
Every body knows the advantage to
be made in cafe of mortgage, by fore-
clofing or forcing a fale : and that this
advantage is not uncommonly looked
out for, will, I believe, hardly be doubt-
ed by any one, who has had any occafion to obferve the courfe of bufinefs
in the court of Chancery.

In fhort, fo long as a prodigal has any
thing to pledge, or to difpofe of, whether in poffeffion, or even in reverfion,
whether of a certain or even of a contingent nature, I fee not, how he can receive the fmalleft benefit, from any
laws that are, or can be made to fix the
rate of intereft. For, fuppofe the law
to be efficacious as far as it goes, and
that the prodigal can find none of thofe

mon-

monſters called uſurers to deal with
him, does he lie quiet ? No ſuch thing :
he goes on and gets the money he
wants, by ſelling his intereſt inſtead of
borrowing. He goes on, I ſay : for if
he has prudence enough to ſtop him
any where, he is not that ſort of man,
whom it can be worth while for the law
to attempt ſtopping by ſuch means.
It is plain enough then, I take it, that
to a prodigal thus circumſtanced, the
law cannot be of any ſervice ; on the
contrary, it may, and in many caſes
muſt, be of diſſervice to him, by denying him the option of a reſource
which, how diſadvantageous foever,
could not well have proved more ſo,
but would naturally have proved leſs

ſo,

fo, than thofe which it leaves ftill open
to him.   But of this hereafter.

I now come to the only remaining
clafs of prodigals, viz. thofe who have
nothing that can be called a fecurity to
offer.   Thefe, I take it, are not more
likely to get money upon an extraordinary rate of intereft, than an ordinary cne.   Perfons who either feel, or
find reafons for pretending to feel, a
friendfhip for the borrower, can not
take of him more than the ordinary
rate of intereft : perfons, who have
no fuch motive for lending him, will
not lend him at all.   If they know him
for what he is, that will prevent them
of courfe: and even though they fhould
know

know nothing of him by any other
circumſtance, the very circumſtance of
his not being able to find a friend to
truſt him at the higheſt ordinary rate,
will be ſufficient reaſon to a ſtranger for
looking upon him as a man, who, in
the judgment of his friends, is not likely to pay.

The **way** that prodigals run into
debt, after they have ſpent their ſub-
ſtance, is, I take it, by borrowing of
their friends and acquaintance, at ordinary intereſt, or more commonly at no
intereſt, ſmall ſums, ſuch as each man
may be content to loſe, or be aſhamed
to aſk real ſecurity for ; and as prodi-
digals

digals have generally an extenfive acquaintance (extenfive acquaintance being at once the caufe and effect of prodigality) the fum total of the money a man may thus find means to
fquander, may be confiderable, though
each fum borrowed may, relatively to
the circumftances of the lender, have
been inconfiderable. This I take to
be the race which prodigals, who have
fpent their all, run at prefent, under the
prefent fyftem of reftraining laws : and
this, and no other, I take it, would be
the race they would run, were thofe
laws out of the way.

Another confideration there is, I
think, which will compleat your conviction

viction, if is was not compleat before, of the inefficacy of thefe laws, as
to the putting any fort of reftraint upon
prodigality. This is, that there is another fet of people from whom prodigals get what they want, and always
will get it, fo long as credit lafts, in
fpite of all laws againft high intereft ;
and, fhould they find it neceffary, at
an expence more than equal to any ex-
cefs of intereft they might otherwife
have to give. I mean the tradefmen
who deal in the goods they want.
Every body knows it is much eafier to
get goods than money. People truft
goods upon much flenderer fecurity
than they do money : it is very natural
they fhould do fo : ordinary profit of
                                    trade

trade upon the whole capital employed in a man's trade, even after the expence of warehouse-rent, journeymen's wages, and other such general charges, are taken into the account, and set against it, is at least equal to double interest ; say 10 per cent. Ordinary profit upon any particular parcel of goods must therefore be a great deal more, say at least triple interest, 15 per cent. : in the way of trading, then, a man can afford to be at least three times as adventurous, as he can in the way of lending, and with equal prudence. So long, then, as a man is looked upon as one who will pay, he can much easier get the goods he wants, than he could the money to buy them

C 3   with,

with, though he were content to give
for it twice, or even thrice the ordinary
rate of intereſt.

Suppoſing any body, for the ſake of
extraordinary gain, to be willing to run
the riſk of ſupplying him, although
they did not look upon his perſonal
ſecurity to be equal to that of another
man, and for the ſake of the extraordinary profit to run the extraordinary
riſk ; in the trader, in ſhort in every
ſort of trader whom he was accuſtom-
ed to deal with in his ſolvent days, he
ſees a perſon who may accept of any
rate of profit, without the ſmalleſt danger from any laws that are, or can be
made againſt uſury. How idle, then,
to think of ſtopping a man from making

ing fix, or feven, or eight per cent. intereft, when, if he chufes to run a rifk
proportionable, he may in this way
make thirty or forty per cent. or any
rate you pleafe. And as to the prodigal, if he cannot get what he wants
upon thefe terms, what chance is
there of his getting it upon any terms,
fuppofing the laws againft ufury to
be away ? This then is another
way, in which, inftead of ferving,
it injures him, by narrowing his
option, and driving him from a market which might have proved lefs difadvantageous, to a more difadvantageous one

As

As far as prodigality, then, is con‑
cerned, I muſt confeſs, I cannot ſee
the uſe of ſtopping the current of
expenditure in this way at the foſſet,
when there are ſo many unprevent‑
able ways of letting it run out at the
bung-hole.

Whether any harm is done to ſo‑
ciety, upon the whole, by letting ſo
much money drop at once out of the
pockets of the prodigal, who would
have gone on waſting it, into the till
of the frugal tradeſman, who will lay it
up, is not worth the enquiry for the pre‑
ſent purpoſe : what is plain is, that, ſo
far as the ſaving the prodigal for paying at an extraordinaty rate from what
he gets to ſpend, is the object of the
law,

law, that object is not at all promoted,
by fixing the rate of interest upon money borrowed.   On the contrary, if the
law has any effect, it runs counter to
that object : since, were he to borrow,
it would only be, in as far as he could
borrow at a rate inferior to that at which
otherwife he would be obliged to buy.
Preventing his borrowing at an extra
rate, may have the effect of increasing
his diftrefs, but cannot have the effect
of leffening it : allowing his borrowing
at fuch a rate, might have the effect of
leffening his diftrefs, but could not have
the effect of increasing it.

To put a ftop to prodigality, if indeed it be worth while, I know but of
one effectual courfe that can be taken,

in

in addition to the incompleat and infufficient. courfes at prefent practicable,
and that is, to put the convicted prodigal under an *interdict*, as was practifed
formerly among the Romans, and is
ftill practifed among the French, and
other nations who have taken the Ro-
man law for the ground work of their
own. But to difcufs the expediency,
or fketch out the details of fuch an inftitution, belongs not to the prefent purpofe.

LETTER

LETTER IV.

*Reasons for Restraint.—Protection of In-
digence.*

BESIDES prodigals, there are three
other classes of persons, and but three,
for whose security I can conceive
these restrictive laws to have been de-
signed. I mean the indigent, the rash-
ly enterprizing, and the simple : those
whose pecuniary necessities may dif-
pose them to give an interest above the
ordinary

ordinary rate, rather than not have it,
and thofe who, from rafhnefs, may be
difpofed to venture upon giving fuch a
rate, or from careleffnefs combined with
ignorance, may be difpofed to acquiefce
in it.

In fpeaking of thefe three different
claffes of perfons, I muft beg leave to
confider one of them at a time: and
accordingly, in fpeaking of the indigent, I muft confider indigence in the
firft place as untinctured with fimplicity. On this occafion, I may fuppofe,
and ought to fuppofe, no particular
defect in a man's judgment, or his
temper, that fhould miflead him, more
than the ordinary run of men. He
knows

knows what is his intereſt as well as they do, and is as well diſpoſed and able to purſue it as they are.

I have already intimated, what I think is undeniable, that there are no one or two or other limited number of rates of intereſt, that can be equally ſuited to the unlimited number of ſituations, in reſpect of the degree of *exigency*, in which a man is liable to find himſelf: inſomuch, that to the ſituation of a man, who by the uſe of money can make for example 11 per cent. ſix per cent is as well adapted, as 5 per cent is to the ſituation of him who can make but 10; to that of him who can make 12 per cent. ſeven, and ſo on. So, in the

caſe

cafe of his wanting it to fave himfelf
from a lofs, (which is that which is
moft likely to be in view under the
name of *exigency)* if that lofs would
amount to 11 per cent. 6 per cent. is
as well adapted to his fituation, as 5
per cent. would be to the fituation of
him, who had but a lofs amounting to
ten per cent. to fave himfelf from by
the like means. And in any cafe,
though, in proporrion to the amount
of the lofs, the rate of intereft were
even fo great, as that the clear faving
fhould not amount to more than one
per cent. or any fraction per cent. yet
fo long as it amounted to any thing, he
would be juft fo much the better for
borrowing, even on fuch comparative-
ly

ly difadvantageous terms. If, inftead
of gain, we put any other kind of benefit or advantage—if, inftead of lofs,
we put any other kind of mifchief or
inconvenience, of equal value, the refult will be the fame.

A man is in one of thefe fituations,
fuppofe, in which it would be for his
advantage to borrow. But his cercum-
ftances are fuch, that it would not be
worth any body's while to lend him,
at the higheft rate which it is propofed
the law fhould allow ; in fhort, he cannot get it at that rate. If he thought
he *could* get it at that rate, moft furely
he would not give a higher ; he may be
trufted for that· for by the fuppofition
                                        he

he has nothing defective in his under-
ftanding. But the fact is, he cannc
get it at that lower rate. At a higher
rate, however, he could get it : and at
that rate, though higher, it would be
worth his while to get it : fo he judges,
who has nothing to hinder him from
judging right; who has every motive
and every means for forming a right
judgment; who has every motive and
every means for informing himfelf of
the circumftances, upon which rectitude of judgment, in the cafe in queftion, depends. The legiflator, who
knows nothing, nor can know any
thing, of any one of all thefe circumftances, who knows nothing at all
about the matter, comes and fays to
him—

him—" It fignifies nothing ; you fhall
", not have the money : for it would be
" a mifchief to you to borrow it upon
" fuch terms."—And this out of prudence and loving-kindnefs !——There
may be worfe cruelty : but can there
be greater folly ?

The folly of thofe who perfift, as
is fuppofed, without reafon, in not
taking advice, has been much expati-
ated upon.   But the folly of thofe who
perfift, without reafon, in forcing their
advice upon others, has been but little
dwelt upon, though it is, perhaps, the
more frequent, and the more flagrant
of the two.   It is not often that one man
is a better judge for another, than that
other

other is for himſelf, even in caſes where
the adviſer will take the trouble to
make himſelf maſter of as many of the
materials for judging, as are within the
reach of the perſon to be adviſed. But
the legiſlator is not, can not be, in the
poſſeſſion of any one of theſe materials.
—What private, can be equal to ſuch
public folly?

I ſhould now ſpeak of the enterprizing claſs of borrowers: thoſe, who,
when characterized by a ſingle term,
are diſtinguiſhed by the unfavourable
appellation of *projectors:* but in what I
ſhall have to ſay of them, Dr. Smith,
I begin to foreſee, will bear ſo material
a part,

a part, that when I come to enter upon that fubject, I think to take my leave of you, and addrefs myfelf to him.

LET-

———————

L E T T E R   V.

Reasons for Restraint.—Protection of Simplicity.

I Come, lastly, to the case of the simple. Here, in the first place, I think I am by this time entitled to observe, that no simplicity, short of absolute idiotism, can cause the individual to

make

make a more groundlefs judgment,
than the legiflator, who, in the circumftances above ftated, fhould pretend to confine him to any given
rate of intereft, would have made for
him.

Another confideration, equally conclufive, is, that were the legiflator's
judgment ever fo much fuperior to the
individual's, how weak foever that
may be, the exertion of it on this occafion can never be any otherwife than
ufelefs, fo long as there are fo many
fimilar occafions, as there ever muft
be, where the fimplicity of the individual is equally liable to make him

D a fuf-

a fufferer, and on which the legiflator
cannot interpofe with effect, nor has
ever fo much as thought of interpof-
ing.

Buying goods with money, or upon
credit, is the bufinefs of every day :
borrowing money is the bufinefs, only, of fome particular exigency, which,
in comparifon, can occur but feldom.
Regulating the prices of goods in general would be an endlefs tafk; and no
legiflator has ever been weak enough
to think of attempting it. And fuppofing he were to regulate the prices,
what would that fignify for the protection of fimplicity, unlefs he were to
regulate alfo the quantum of what each

man

man fhould buy ? Such quantum is
indeed regulated, or rather means are
taken to prevent buying altogether ;
but in what cafes ? in thofe only where
the weaknefs is adjudged to have arrived at fuch a pitch, as to render a
man utterly unqualified for the manage-
ment of his affairs : in fhort, when it
has arrived at the length of idiocy.

But in what degree foever a man's
weaknefs may expofe him to impofition, he ftands much more expofed to
it, in the way of buying goods, than
in the way of borrowing money. To
be informed, beforehand, of the ordi
nary prices of all forts of things, a man

D 2   may

may have occasion to buy, may be a
task of confiderable variety and extent.
To be informed of the ordinary rate of
intereft, is to be informed of one fingle
fact, too interefting not to have at-
tracted attention, and too fimple to
have efcaped the memory.   A few per
cent. enhancement upon the price of
goods, is a matter that may eafily
enough pafs unheeded ; but a fingle
per cent. beyond the ordinary intereft
of money, is a ftride more confpicuous and ftartling, than many per
cent. upon the price of any kind of
goods.

Even in regard to fubjects, which
by their importance, would, if any,
juftify a regulation of their price, fuch
as for inftance land, I queftion whether

ther there ever was an inftance where,
without fome fuch ground as, on the
one fide fraud, or fuppreffion of facts
neceffary to form a judgment of the
value, or at leaft ignorance of fuch
facts, on the other, a bargain was re-
fcinded, merely becaufe a man had fold
too cheap, or bought too dear.   Were
I to take a fancy to give a hundred
years purchafe inftead of thirty, for a
piece of land, rather than not have it.
I don't think there is any court in England, or indeed any where elfe, that
would interpofe to hinder me, much lefs
to punifh the feller with the lofs of three
times the purchafe money, as in the
cafe of ufury.   Yet when I had got my
piece of land, and paid my money, re-
pentance, were the law ever fo well

dif-

difpofed to affift me, might be unavail-
ing for the feller might have fpent
the money, or gone off with it. But,
in the cafe of borrowing money, it is
the borrower always, who, according to the indefinite, or fhort term for
which money is lent, is on the fafe fide :
any imprudence he may have com-
mitted with regard to the rate of
intereft, may be corrected at any
time : if I find I have given too high
an intereft to one man, I have no
more to do than to borrow of another
at a lower rate, and pay off the firft :
if I can not find any body to lend me
at a lower, there cannot be a more

certain

certain proof that the firſt was not in reality too high. But of this here-after.

LETTER

LETTER VI.

Mischiefs of the anti-usurious Laws.

IN the preceding letters, I have ex-
amined all the modes I can think of,
in which the reſtraints, impoſed by the
laws againſt uſury, can have been fan-
cied to be of ſervice.

I hope it appears by this time, that
there are no ways in which thoſe laws
can do any good. But there are ſeveral

veral, in which they can not but do mifchief.

The firſt, I ſhall mention, is that of precluding ſo many people altogether, from the getting the money they ſtand in need of, to anſwer their reſpective exigencies. Think what a diſtreſs it would produce, were the liberty of borrowing denied to every body: denied to thoſe who have ſuch ſecurity to offer, as renders the rate of intereſt, they have to offer, a ſufficient inducement, for a man who has money, to truſt them with it. Juſt that ſame ſort of diſtreſs is produced, by denying that liberty to ſo many people, whoſe ſecurity, though, if they were

D 5   permitted

permitted to add fomething to that rate, it would be fufficient, is rendered infufficient by their being denied that liberty. Why the misfortune, of not being poffeffed of that arbitarily exacted degree of fecurity, fhould be made a ground for fubjecting a man to a hardfhip, which is not impofed on thofe who are free from that misfortune, is more than I can fee. To difcriminate the former clafs from the latter I can fee but this one circumftance, viz. that their neceffity is greater. This it is by the very fuppofition: for were it not, they could not be what they are fuppofed to be, willing to give more to be relieved from it. In this point of view then, the fole

ten-

tendency of the law is, to heap diftrefs
upon diftrefs.

A fecond mifchief is, that of rendering the terms fo much the worfe,
to a multitude of thofe, whofe circumftances exempt them from being precluded altogether from getting the
money they have occafion for. In
this cafe, the mifchief, though neceffarily lefs intenfe than in the other, is
much more palpable and confpicuous.
Thofe who cannot borrow may get
what they want, fo long as they have
any thing to fell. But while out of
loving kindnefs, or whatfoever other
motive, the law precludes a man from
borrowing, upon terms which he deems

too

too difadvantageous, it does not pre-
clude him from *felling*, upon any
terms, howfoever difadvantageous.
Every body knows that forced fales
are attended with a lofs: and, to this
lofs, what would be deemed a moft
extravagant intereft bears in general no
proportion.   When a man's moveables
are taken in execution, they are, I believe, pretty well fold, if, after all expences paid, the produce amounts to
two thirds of what it would coft to replace
them.   In this way the providence and
loving-kindnefs of the law cofts him 33
per cent. and no more, fuppofing, what
is feldom the cafe, that no more of the
effects are taken than what is barely
neceffary

neceffary to make up the money due.
If in her negligence and weaknefs,
fhe were to fuffer him to offer 11 per
cent. per annum for forbearance, it
would be three years before he paid
what he is charged with, in the firft inftance, by her wifdom.

Such being the kindnefs done by the
law to the owner of moveables, let us
fee how it fares with him who has an
intereft in immoveables. Before the
late war, 30 years purchafe for land
might be reckoned, I think it is pretty well agreed, a medium price. During the diftrefs produced by the war,
lands, which it was neceffary fhould be
fold, were fold at 20, 18, nay, I believe,

lieve, in fome inftances, even fo low as
15 years purchafe. If I do not mif-
recollect, I remember inftances of
lands put up to public auction, for
which nobody bid fo high as fifteen.
In many inftances, villas, which had
been bought before the war, or at the
beginning of it, and, in the interval,
had been improved rather than impair-
ed, fold for lefs than half, or even the
quarter, of what they had been bought
for. I dare not here for my part pretend to be exact : but on this paffage,
were it worth their notice, Mr. Skin-
ner, or Mr. Chriftie, could furnifh
very inftructive notes. Twenty-years
purchafe, inftead of thirty, I may be
allowed to take, at leaft for illuftration.

tion. An eftate then of 100l. a year,
clear of taxes, was devifed to a man,
charged, fuppofe, with 1500l. with
intereft till the money fhould be paid.
Five per cent. intereft, the utmoft
which could be accepted from the
owner, did not anfwer the incumbran-
cer's purpofe: he chofe to have the
money. But 6 per cent. perhaps,
would have anfwered his purpofe, if
not, moft certainly it would have anfwered the purpofe of fomebody elfe:
for multitudes there all along were, whofe
purpofes were anfwered by five per cent.
The war lafted, I think, feven years: the
depreciation of the value of land did not
take place immediately: but as, on the
other hand, neither did it immediately
recover

recover its former price upon the peace, if indeed it has even yet recovered it we may put feven years for the time, during which it would be more advantageous to pay this extraordinary rate of inte-reft than fell the land, and during which, accordingly, this extraordinary rate of intereft would have had to run. One per cent. for feven years, is not quite of equal worth to feven per cent. the firft year: fay, however, that it is. The eftate, which before the war was worth thirty years, pur-chafe, that is 3000l. and which the devifor had given to the devifee for that value, being put up to fale, fetch-ed but 20 years purchafe, 2000l. At the end of that period it would

have

have fetched its original value, 3000l.
Compare, then, the fituation of the
devifee at the feven years end, under the
law, with what it would have been,
without the law. In the former cafe,
the land felling for 20 years purchafe,
i. e. 2000 l. what he would have after paying the 1500 l. is 500 l. ; which,
with the intereft of that fum, at 5 per
cent. for feven years, viz. 175 l. makes,
at the end of that feven years, 675 l.
In the other cafe, paying 6 per cent.
on the 1500 l. that is 90 l. a year, and
receiving all that time the rent of the
land, viz. 100 l. he would have had,
at the feven years end, the amount of
the remaining ten pounds during that
period, that is 70 l. in addition to his
1000 l.—675 l. fubftracted from 1070 l.

leaves

leaves 395 l. This 395 l. then, is what
he lofes out of 1070 l. almoſt 37 per
cent. of his capital, by the loving kindnefs of the law. Make the calculations, and you will find, that, by preventing him from borrowing the money
at 6 per cent. intereſt, it makes him
nearly as much a fufferer as if he had
borrowed it at ten.

What I have ſaid hitherto, is confined to the cafe of thoſe who have
preſent value to give, for the money
they ſtand in need of. If they have
no ſuch value, then, if they fucceed in
purchaſing affiſtance upon any terms,
it muſt be in breach of the law ; their
lenders expoſing themſelves to its ven-
geance :

geance : for I fpeak not here of the ac-
cidental cafe, of its being fo conftruct-
ed as to be liable to evafion. But,
even in this cafe, the mifchievous influence of the law ftill purfues them;
aggravating the very mifchief it pretends to remedy. Though it be inefficacious in the way in which the legiflator wifhes to fee it efficacious, it is
efficacious in the way oppofite to that
in which he would wifh to fee it fo.
The effect of it is, to raife the rate of
intereft, higher than it would be otherwife, and that in two ways. In the
firft place, a man muft, in common
prudence, as Dr. Smith obferves, make
a point of being indemnified, not only
for whatfoever extraordinary rifk it is

that

that he runs independently of the law, but for the very rifk occafioned by the law : he muft be *infured*, as it were, againft the law.   This caufe would operate, were there even as many per- fons ready to lend upon the illegal rate, as upon the legal.   But this is not the cafe : a great number of perfons are, of courfe, driven out of this com- petition, by the danger of the bufinefs ; and another great number, by the dif- repute which, under cover of thefe pro- hibitory laws or otherwife, has faften- ed itfelf upon the name of ufurer.   So many perfons, therefore, being driven out of the trade, it happens in this branch, as it muft neceffarily in every other, that thofe who remain have the

lefs

lefs to with-hold them from advancing
their terms ; and without confederating,
(for it muft be allowed that confedera-
cy in fuch a cafe is plainly impoffible)
each one will find it eafier to pufh his
advantage up to any given degree of
exorbitancy, than he would, if there
were a greater number of perfons of the
fame ftamp to refort to.

As to the cafe, where the law is fo
worded as to be liable to be evaded,
in this cafe it is partly inefficacious and
nugatory, and partly mifchievous. It
is nugatory, as to all fuch, whofe confidence of its being fo is perfect : it is
mifchievous, as before, in regard to all
fuch who fail of poffeffing that perfect
confi-

confidence. If the borrower can find
nobody at all who has confidence
enough to take advantage of the flaw,
he ftands precluded from all affiftance,
as before : and, though he fhould, yet
the lender's terms muft neceffarily run
the higher, in proportion to what his
confidence wants of being perfect. It
is not likely that it fhould be perfect :
it is ftill lefs likely that he fhould acknowledge it fo to be : it is not likely,
at leaft as matters ftand in England,
that the worft-penned law made for
this purpofe fhould be altogether defti-
tute of effect : and while it has any,
that effect, we fee, muft be in one way
or other mifchievous.

I have

I have already hinted at the difrepute,
the ignominy, the reproach, which prejudice, the caufe and the effect of thefe
reftrictive laws has heaped upon that
perfectly innocent and even meritorious
clafs of men, who, not more for their
own advantage than to the relief of
the diftreffes of their neighbour, may
have ventured to break through thefe
reftraints. It is certainly not a matter
of indifference, that a clafs of perfons,
who, in every point of view in which
their conduct can be placed, whether.
in relation to their own intereft, or in
relation to that of the perfons whom
they have to deal with, as well on the
fcore of prudence, as on that of beneficence, (and of what ufe is even benevolence,

volence, but in as far as it is productive
of beneficence?) deferve praife rather
than cenfure, fhould be claffed with
the abandoned and profligate, and
loaded with a degree of infamy, which
is due to thofe only whofe conduct is
in its tendency the moft oppofite to
their own.

"This fuffering," it may be faid,
"having already been taken account
of, is not to be brought to account a
fecond time: they are aware, as you
yourfelf obferve, of this inconvenience,
and have taken care to get fuch amends
for it, as they themfelves look upon as
fufficient." True.: but it is fure that
the compenfation, fuch as it is, will always

ways, in the event, have proved a suffi-
cient one? Is there no room here for
miscalculation? May there not be un-
expected, unlooked-for incidents, suffi-
cient to turn into bitterness the utmost
satisfaction which the difference of
pecuniary emolument could afford?
For who can see to the end of that in-
exhaustible train of consequences that
are liable to ensue from the loss of repu-
tation? Who can fathom the abyss of
infamy? At any rate, this article of
mischief, if not an addition in its
quantity to the others above-noticed,
is at least distinct from them in its
nature, and as such ought not to be
overlooked.

E   Nor

Nor is the event of the execution of
the law by any means an unexampled
one : feveral fuch, at different times,
have fallen within my notice. Then
comes abfolute perdition : lofs of cha-
racter, and forfeiture, not of three
times the extra-intereft, which formed
the profit of the offence, but of three
times the principal, which gave occafion
to it.

The laft article I have to mention in
the account of mifchief, is, the corrup-
tive influence, exercifed by thefe laws,
on the morals of the people ; by the
pains they take, and cannot but take,

to

to give birth to treachery and ingra-
titude. To purchafe a poffibility of
being enforced, the law neither has
found, nor, what is very material, muft
it ever hope to find, in this cafe, any
other expedient, than that of hiring a
man to break his engagement, and to
crufh the hand that has been reached
out to help him. In the cafe of in-
formers in general, there has been no
troth plighted, nor benefit received.
In the cafe of real criminals invited by
rewards to inform againft accomplices,
it is by fuch *breach* of faith that fociety
is held together, as in other cafes by
the *obfervance* of it. In the cafe of real

E 2   crimes,

crimes, in proportion as their mifchievoufnefs is apparent, what cannot
but be manifeft even to the criminal,
s, that it is by the adherence to his
engagement that he would do an injury
to fociety, and, that by the breach of
fuch engagement, inftead of doing mifchief he is doing good : in the cafe of
ufury this is what no man can know,
and what one can fcarcely think it poffible for any man, who, in the cha-
racter of the borrower, has been concerned in fuch a tranfaction, to imagine.
He knew that, even in his own judg
ment, the engagement was a beneficial
                                    one

one to himſelf, or he would not have en-
tered into it: and nobody elſe but the
lender is affected by it

LETTER

LETTER VII.

Efficacy of anti-usurious Laws.

BEFORE I quit altogether the
confideration of the cafe in which a law,
made for the purpofe of limiting the
rate of intereft, may be inefficacious
with regard to that end, I can not forbear

bear taking fome further notice of a
paffage already alluded of Dr. Smith's:
becaufe, to my apprehenfion, that
paffage feems to throw upon the fubject a degree of obfcurity, which I could
wifh to fee cleared up, in a future edition of that valuable work.

" No law" fays he*, " can re-
" duce the common rate of inte-
" reft below the loweft ordinary mar-
" ket rate, at the time when that law
" was made. Notwithftanding the
" edict of 1766, by which the French

---

* B. ii. c. 10. vol. ii. p. 45. edit. 8vo. 1784.

" king

" king attempted to reduce the rate of
" intereſt from five to four per cent.
" money continued to be lent in
" France at five per cent. the law
being evaded in ſeveral different
ways."

As to the general poſition, if ſo it be,
ſo much, according to me, the better :
but I muſt confeſs I do not ſee why this
ſhould be the caſe. It is for the purpoſe of proving the truth of this general poſition, that the fact of the inefficacy of this attempt ſeems to be adduced : for no other proof is adduced
but this. But, taking the fact for
granted, I do not ſee how it can be
ſufficient to ſupport the inference. The
law,

law, we are told at the fame time, was evaded : but we are not told how it came to be open to evafion. It might be owing to a particular defect in the penning of that particular law : or, what comes to the fame thing, in the provifions made for carrying it into execution. In either cafe, it affords no fupport to the general pofition : nor can that pofition be a juft one, unlefs it were fo in the cafe where every provifion had been made, that could be made, for giving efficacy to the law. For the pofition to be true, the cafe muft be, that the law would ftill be broken, even after every means of what can properly be called *evafion* had been removed. True or untrue, the

E 5   pofition

pofition is certainly not felf-evident
enough to be received without proof :
yet nothing is adduced in proof of it,
but the fact above-noticed, which we
fee amounts to no fuch thing. What
is more, I fhould not expect to find
it capable of proof. I do not fee,
what it is, that fhould render the
law incapable of " reducing the com-
" mon rate of intereft below the lowest-
" ordinary market rate," but fuch a
ftate of things, fuch a combination of
circumftances, as fhould afford obftacles equally powerful, or nearly fo, to
the efficacy of the law againft all
higher rates. For deftroying the law's
efficacy altogether, I know of nothing
that

that could ferve, but a refolution on the part of all perfons any way privy not to inform : but by fuch a refolution any higher rate is juft as effectually protected as any lower one. Suppofe it, ftrictly fpeaking, univerfal, and the law muft in all inftances be equally inefficacious ; all rates of intereft are equally free ; and the ftate of men's dealings in this way juft what it would be, were there no law at all upon the fubject. But in this cafe, the pofition, in as far as it limits the inefficacy of the law to thofe rates which are below the " loweft ordinary market rate," is not true. For my part, I cannot conceive how any fuch univerfal refolution
tion

tion could have been maintained, or could ever be maintained, without an open concert, and as open a rebellion againſt government ; nothing of which ſort appears to have taken place : and, as to any particular confederacies, they are as capable of protecting any higher rates againſt the prohibition, as any lower ones.

Thus much indeed muſt be admitted, that the low rate in queſtion, viz. that which was the loweſt ordinary market rate immediately before the making of the law, is likely to come in for the protection of the public againſt the law, more frequently than

any

any other rate. That muſt be the
caſe on two accounts : firſt, becauſe by
being of the number of the ordinary
rates, it was, by the ſuppoſition, more
frequent than any extraordinary ones :
ſecondly, beeauſe the diſrepute annexed to the idea of uſury, a force which
might have more or leſs efficacy in ex-
cluding, from the protection above
ſpoken of, ſuch extraordinary rates,
cannot well be ſuppoſed to apply itſelf,
or at leaſt not in equal degree, to this
low and ordinary rate. A lender has
certainly leſs to ſtop him from taking
a rate, which may be taken without
diſrepute, than from taking one, which
a man could not take without ſubject-
ing

ing himfelf to that inconvenience : nor
is it likely, that men's imaginations and
fentiments fhould teftify fo fudden an
obfequioufnefs to the law, as to ftamp
difrepute to-day, upon a rate of intereft, to which no fuch accompaniment
had ftood annexed the day before.

Were I to be afked how I imagined the cafe ftood in the particular inftance referred to by Dr. Smith ; judging from his account of it, affifted by
general probabilities, I fhould anfwer
thus :—The law, I fhould fuppofe, was,
not·fo penned as to be altogether proof
againft evafion.   In many inftances,
of which it is impoffible any account
fhould

fhould have been taken, it was indeed
conformed to : in fome of thofe inftances, people who would have lent
otherwife, abftained from lending altogether ; in others of thofe inflances,
people lent their money at the reduced
legal rate.   In other inftances again,
the law was broken : the lenders truft-
ing, partly to expedients recurred to
for evading it, partly to the good faith
and honour of thofe whom they had
to deal with : in this clafs of inftances
it was natural for the two reafons
above fuggefted, that thofe where the
old legal rate was adhered to, fhould
have been the moft numerous.   From
the circumftance not only of their
                                    number,

number, but of their more direct re-
pugnancy to the particular recent law
in queftion, they would naturally be
the moft taken notice of. And this, I
take it, was the foundation in point
of fact for the Doctor's general pofition above mentioned, that " no law
" *can* reduce the common rate of inte-
" reft below the loweft ordinary mar-
" ket rate, at the time when that law
" was made."

In England, as far as I can truft my
judgment and imperfect general recollection of the purport of the laws relative to this matter, I fhould not fuppofe that the above pofition would
prove

prove true. That there is no fuch thing as any palpable and univerfally notorious, as well as univerfally practicable receipt for that purpofe, is manifeft from the examples which, as I have already mentioned, every now and then occur, of convictions upon thefe ftatutes. Two fuch receipts, indeed, I fhall have occafion to touch upon prefently : but they are either not obvious enough in their nature, or too troublefome or not extenfive enough in their application, to have defpoiled the law altogether of its terrors or of its preventive efficacy.

In

In the country in which I am writing, the whole fyftem of laws on this fubject is perfectly, and very happily, inefficacious. The rate fixed by law is 5 per cent. : many people lend money ; and nobody at that rate : the loweft ordinary rate, upon the very beft real fecurity, is 8 per cent. : 9, and even 10, upon fuch fecurity, are common. Six or feven may have place, now and then, between relations or other particular friends : becaufe, now and then, a man may choofe to make a prefent of one or two per cent. to a perfon whom he means to favour.

The

The contract is renewed from year to
year : for a thousand roubles, the borrower in his written contract, obliges
himself to pay at the end of the year
one thousand and fifty.   Before witnesses, he receives his thousand roubles : and, without witnesses, he immediately pays back his 30 roubles, or
his 40 roubles, or whatever the sum
may be, that is necessary to bring the
real rate of interest to the rate verbally
agreed on.

This contrivance, I take it, would
not do in England : but why it would
not,

not, is a queſtion which it would
be in vain for me to pretend, at
this diſtance from all authorities, to
diſcuſs.

LETTER

———————

L E T T E R   VIII.

Virtual Usury allowed.

Having proved, as I hope, by this time, the utter impropriety of the law's limiting the rate of interest, in every cafe that can be conceived, it may be rather matter of curiofity, than any thing elfe, to enquire, how far the law, on this head, is confiftent with it-

self,

felf, and with any principles upon which
it can have built.

1. *Drawing and re-drawing* is a
practice, which it will be fufficient
here to hint at.   It is perfectly well
known to all merchants, and may be
fo to all who are not merchants, by
confulting Dr. Smith.   In this way
he has fhewn how money may be, and
has been, taken up, at fo high a rate,
as 13 or 14 per cent. a rate nearly
three times as high as the utmoft
which the law profeffes to allow.   The
extra intereft is in this cafe mafked under the names of *commiffion*, and price
of *exchange*.   The commiffion is but
fmall

ſmall upon each loan, not more, I
think, than ½ per cent. : cuſtom having ſtretched ſo far but no farther, it
might be thought dangerous, perhaps,
to venture upon any higher allowance
under that name. The charge, being
repeated a number of times in the
courſe of the year, makes up in fre-
quency what it wants in weight. The
tranſaction is by this ſhift rendered
more troubleſome, indeed, but not leſs
practicable, to ſuch parties as are
agreed about it. But if uſury is good
for merchants, I don't very well ſee
what ſhould make it bad for every
body elſe.

2. At

2. At this diſtance from all the fountains of legal knowledge, I will not pretend to ſay, whether the practice of *ſelling accepted bills* at an under value, would hold good againſt all attacks. It ſtrikes my recollection as a pretty common one, and I think it could not be brought under any of the penal ſtatutes againſt uſury. The adequatenefs of the conſideration might, for aught I know, be attacked with ſucceſs, in a court of equity ; or, perhaps, if there were ſufficient evidence (which the agreement of the parties might eaſily prevent) by an action at common law, for money had and received. If the practice be really proof againſt all attacks, it ſeems to

afford

afford an effectual, and pretty commodious method of evading the restrictive laws. The only restraint is,
that it requires the assistance of a third
person, a friend of the borrower's ; as
for instance : *B*, the real borrower,
wants 100l. and finds *U*, a usurer,
who is willing to lend it to him, at 10
per cent. *B.* has *F*, a friend, who has
not the money himself to lend him,
but is willing to stand security for
him, to that amount. *B.* therefore
draws upon *F*, and *F.* accepts, a bill
of 100l. at 5 per cent. interest, pay-
able at the end of a twelvemonth
from the date. *F.* draws a like bill
upon *B.* : each sells his bill to *U.* for

F   fifty

fifty pounds; and it is endorfed to *U.*
accordingly.   The 50l. that *F.* receives, he delivers over without any
confideration to *B.* This tranfaction,
if it be a valid one, and if a man can
find fuch a friend, is evidently much
lefs troublefome than the practice of
drawing and re-drawing.   And this,
if it be practicable at all, may be
practifed by perfons of any defcription, concerned or not in trade.
Should the effect of this page be to
fuggeft an expedient, and that a fafe
and commodious one, for evading the
laws againft ufury, to fome, to whom
fuch an expedient might not otherwife
have occurred, it will not lie very hea-
vy upon my confcience.   The prayers
of

of ufurers, whatever efficacy they may
have in lightening the burthen, I hope
I may lay fome claim to.   And I think
you will not now wonder at my faying,
that in the efficacy of fuch prayers I
have not a whit lefs confidence, than in
that of the prayers of any other clafs
of men.

One apology I fhall have to plead
at any rate, that in pointing out thefe
flaws, to the individual who may be
difpofed to creep out at them, I point
them out at the fame time to the legiflator, in whofe power it is to ftop
them up, if in his opinion they require
it.   If, notwithftanding fuch opinion,
he fhould omit to do fo, the blame

F 2   will

will lie, not on my induftry, but on his negligence.

Thefe, it may be faid, fhould they even be fecure and effectual evafions, are ftill but evafions, and, if chargeable upon the law at all, are chargeable not as inconfiftencies but as overfights. Be it fo. Setting thefe afide, then, as expedients practifed or practicable, only behind its back, I will beg leave to remind you of two others, practifed from time to time, under its protection and before its face.

The firft I fhall mention is *pawn-broking*. In this cafe there is the lefs pretence for more than ordinary intereft, inafmuch as the fecurity is, in
this

this cafe, not only equal to, but better than, what it can be in any other : to wit, the prefent poffeffion of a moveable thing, of eafy fale, on which the creditor has the power, and certainly does not want the inclination, to fet fuch price as is moft for his advantage. If there be a cafe in which the allowing of fuch extraordinary intereft is attended with more danger than another, it muft be this : which is fo particularly adapted to the fituation of the loweft poor, that is, of thofe who, on the fcore of indigence or fimplicity, or both, are moft open to impofition. This trade however the law, by regulating, avowedly protects. What the rate of intereft is, which it allows to

F 3 be

be taken in this way, I can not take upon me to remember: but I am much
deceived, if it amounts to lefs than 12
per cent. in the year, and I believe it
amounts to a good deal more. Whether it were 12 per cent. or 1200, I believe would make in practice but little
difference.   What *commiffion* is in the
bufinefs of drawing and re-drawing,
warehoufe-room is, in that of pawnbroking.   Whatever limits then are fet to
the profits of this trade, are fet, I take
it, not by the vigilancy of the law, but,
as in the cafe of other trades, by the
competition amongft the traders.   Of
the other regulations contained in the
acts relative to this fubject I recollect no
reafon to doubt the ufe.

The

The other inftance is that of *bot-tomry* and *refpondentia :* for the two tranfactions, being fo nearly related, may be fpoken of together.   Bottomry is the ufury of pawnbroking : refpon-dentia is ufury at large, but combined in a manner with infurance, and em-ployed in the affiftance of a trade car-ried on by fea.   If any fpecies of ufury is to be condemned, I fee not on what grounds this particular fpecies can be fcreened from the condemnation. " Oh " but" (fays fir William Blackftone, or any body elfe who takes upon himfelf the tafk of finding a reafon for the law) " this is a maritime country, and the " trade, which it carries on by fea, is the " great bulwark of its defence." It is

not

not neceſſary I ſhould here enquire,
whether that branch, which, as Dr.
Smith has ſhewn, is, in every view but
the mere one of defence, leſs beneficial
to a nation, than two others out of the
four branches which comprehend all
trade, has any claim to be preferred
to them in this or any other way.   I
admit, that the liberty which this
branch of trade enjoys, is no more than
what it is perfectly right it ſhould enjoy.
What I want to know is, what there
is in the claſs of men, embarked in
this trade, that ſhould render beneficial
to them, a liberty, which would be
ruinous to every body elſe.   Is it that
ſea adventures have leſs hazard on
them than land adventures ?   or that
the

the fea teaches thofe, who have to deal
with it, a degree of forecaft and reflection which has been denied to land-
men ?

It were eafy enough to give farther
and farther extenfion to this charge of
inconfiftency, by bringing under it the
liberty given to infurance in all its
branches, to the purchafe and fale of
annuities, and of *poft-obits*, in a word
to all cafes where a man is permitted
to take upon himfelf an unlimited degree of rifk, receiving for fo doing an
unlimited compenfation. Indeed I
know not where the want of inftances
would ftop me : for in what part of the
magazine of events, about which hu-

F 5   man

man tranſactions are converſant, is cer-
tainty to be found ? But to this head
of argument, this argument *ad homi-
nem*, as it may be called, the uſe of
which is but ſubſidiary, and which has
more of confutation in it than of per-
ſuaſion or inſtruction, I willingly put
an end.

LETTER

LETTER IX.

Blackſtone conſidered.

I Hope, you are, by this time, at leaſt, pretty much of my opinion, that there is juſt the ſame ſort of harm, and no other, in making the beſt terms one can for one's ſelf in a money loan, as
there

there is in any other fort of bargain.
If you are not, Blackftone however is,
whofe opinion I hope you will allow
to be worth fomething. In fpeaking
of the rate of intereft*, he ftarts a parallel between a bargain for the loan of
money, and a bargain about a horfe,
and pronounces, without hefitation,
that the harm of making too good a
bargain, is juft as great in the one cafe,
as in the other.   As money-lending,
and not horfe-dealing, was, what you
lawyers call, the *principal cafe*, he
drops the horfe bufinefs, as foon as
it has anfwered the purpofe of illuftra-

* B. ii. ch. 13.

tion,

tion, which it was brought to ferve.
But as, in my conception, as well the
reafoning by which he fupports the
decifion, as that by which any body
elfe could have fupported it, is juft as
applicable to the one fort of bargain
as to the other, I will carry on the
parallel a little farther, and give the
fame extent to the reafoning, as to the
pofition which it is made ufe of to
fupport. This extenfion will not be
without its ufe ; for if the pofition,
when thus extended, fhould be found
juft, a practical inference will arife ;
which is, that the benefits of thefe reftraints ought to be extended from
the money-trade to the horfe-trade.
That my own opinion is not favour-

able

able to fuch reftraints in either cafe,
has been fufficiently declared ; but
if more refpectable opinions than
mine are ftill to prevail, they will not
be the lefs refpectable for being confiftent.

The fort of bargain which the
learned commentator has happened to
pitch upon for the illuftration, is indeed, in the cafe illuftrating, as in the
cafe illuftrated, a loan : but as, to my
apprehenfion, loan or fale makes, in
point of reafoning, no fort of difference,
and as the utility of the conclufion will,
in the latter cafe, be more extenfive, I
fhall adapt the reafoning to the more
important bufinefs of felling horfes, inftead

ftead of the lefs important one of lending them.

A circumftance that would render
the extenfion of thefe reftraints to the
horfe-trade more fmooth and eafy, is,
that in the one track, as well as in the
other, the public has already got the
length of calling names. *Jockey-fhip*,
a term of reproach not lefs frequently
applied to the arts of thofe who fell
horfes than to the arts of thofe who
ride them, founds, I take it, to the ear
of many a worthy gentleman, nearly as
bad as *ufury :* and it is well known to
all thofe who put their truft in pro-
verbs, and not lefs to thofe who put
their truft in party, that when we have

got

got a dog to hang who is troublefome
and keeps us at bay, whoever can contrive to faften a bad name to his tail,
has gained more than half the battle.
I now proceed with my application.
The words in *Italics* are my own : all
the reft are Sir William Blackftone's :
and I reftore, at bottom, the words I
was obliged to difcard, in order to make
room for mine.

" To demand an exorbitant price is
" equally contrary to confcience, for
" the loan of a horfe, or for the loan of
" a fum of money : but a reafonable
" equivalent for the temporary incon-
" venience, which the owner may feel
" by the want of it, and for the hazard
" of

" of his losing it entirely, is not more
" immoral in one case than in the
" other. * * * *

" *As to selling horses,* a capital dis-
" tinction must be made, between a
" moderate and an exorbitant profit :
" to the former of which we give the
" name of *horse-dealing**, to the latter
" the truly odious appellation of *joc-*
" *key-ship* † : the former is necessary in
" every civil state, if it were but to ex-
" clude the latter. For, as the whole
" of this matter is well summed up by
" Grotius, if the compensation allowed
" by law does not exceed the propor-

* interest.　　† usury.

" tion

" tion of the *inconvenience which it is to*
" *the seller of the horse to part with it**,
" or the want *which the buyer has of it†*
" its allowance is neither repugnant to
" the revealed law, nor to the natural
" law : but if it exceeds thefe bounds,
" it is then an oppreffive *jockey-ship‡* :
" and though the municipal laws may
" give it impunity, they never can
" make it juft.

" We fee that the exorbitance or
" moderation of *the price given for a*
" *horfe* § depends upon two circum-
" ftances : upon the inconvenience of

---

* hazard run. † felt by the loan. ‡ ufury.
§ intereft for the money lent.

" parting

" parting with *the horfe one has**, and the
" hazard of not *being able to meet with*
" *fuch another* †. The inconvenience to
" individuals, *fellers of horfes*‡, can ne-
" ver be eftimated by laws ; the *gene-*
" *ral price for horfes*§ muft depend there-
" fore upon the ufual or general incon-
" venience. This refults entirely from
" the quantity of *horfes*‖ in the king-
" dom : for the more *horfes*¶ there are
" *running about* * in any nation, the
" greater fuperfluity there will be be-
" yond what is neceffary to carry on the

** it for the prefent. † lofing it entirely.
‡ lenders. § rate of general intereft. ‖ money.
¶ fpecie. ** circulating.*

" bufinefs.

" bufinefs of the *mail coaches*†† and the
" common concerns of life.   In every
" nation or public community there is
" a certain quantity of horfes‡‡ then
" neceffary, which a perfon well fkill-
" ed in political arithmetic might per-
" haps calculate as exactly as a private
" *horfe-dealer* * can the demand for run-
" ning *horfes in his own ftables*† :   all
" above this neceffary quantity may be
" fpared, or lent, *or fold*, without much
" inconvenience to the refpective lend-
" ers or *fellers :* and the greater the na-
" tional fuperfluity is, the more nume-
" rous will be the *fellers* ‡, and the lower

†† exchange.   ‡‡ Money.   * banker.
† cafh in his own fhop.   ‡ lenders.

" ought

" ought *the national price of horfe-flefh**
" to be : but where there are not enough,
" or barely enough *fpare horfes*† to an-
" fwer the ordinary ufes of the public,
" *horfe flefh*‡ will be proportionably
" high : for *fellers*‖ will be but few, as
" few can fubmit to the inconvenience
" of felling§."—So far the learned commentator.

I hope by this time you are worked
up to a proper pitch of indignation, at
the neglect and inconfiftency betrayed

• the rate of the national intereft. † circulating cafh. ‡ intereft. ‖ lenders. § lending.

by

by the law, in not fuppreffing this fpecies of jockey-fhip, which it would
be fo eafy to do, only by fixing the
price of horfes.   Nobody is lefs difpofed than I am to be uncharitable :
but when one thinks of the 1500 l.
taken for Eclipfe, and 2000 l. for
Rockingham, and fo on, who can avoid
being fhocked, to think how little regard thofe who took fuch enormous
prices muft have had for " the law
" of revelation and the law of na-
" ture ?" Whoever it is that is to
move for the municipal law, not long
ago talked of, for reducing the rate
of intereft, whenever that motion is
made, then would be the time for one

of

of the Yorkſhire members to get up, and move, by way of addition, for a clauſe for fixing and reducing the price of horſes. I need not expatiate on the uſefulneſs of that valuable ſpecies of cattle, which might have been as cheap as aſſes before now, if our lawgivers had been as mindful of their duty in the ſuppreſſion of *jockey-ſhip*, as they have been in the ſuppreſſion of *uſury*.

It may be ſaid, againſt fixing the price of horſe fleſh, that different horſes may be of different values. I anſwer—and I think I ſhall ſhew you as much, when I come to touch upon the ſubject of champerty—not more
diffe-

different than the values which the ufe of the fame fum of money may be of to different perfons, on different occafions.

LETTER

_____

LETTER X.

Grounds of the Prejudices against Ufury.

IT is one thing, to find reafons why it is *fit* a law *fhould* have been made: it is another, to find the reafons why it *was* made: in other words, it is one thing to juftify a law: it is another thing to account for its exiftence. In the prefent inftance, the former tafk, if the obfervations I have been trou-

G   bling

bling you with are juft, is an impoffible one.   The other, though ·not
neceffary for conviction, may contri-
bute fomething perhaps in the way of
fatisfaction.   To trace an error to its
fountain head, fays. lord Coke, is to
refute it; and many men there are who,
till they have received this fatisfaction,
be the error what it may, cannot prevail upon themfelves to part with it.
" If our anceftors have been all along
" under a miftake, how came they to
" have fallen into it?" is a queftion
that naturally prefents itfelf upon all
fuch occafions.   The cafe is, that in
matters of law more efpecially, fuch is
the dominion of authority over our
minds, and fuch the prejudice it creates
in favour of whatever inftitution it has
                                            taken

taken under its wing, that, after all
manner of reafons that can be thought
of, in favour of the inftitution, have
been fhewn to be infufficient, we ftill
cannot forbear looking to fome unaf-
fignable and latent reafon for its effi-
cient caufe.   But if, inftead of any fuch
reafon, we can find a caufe for it in
fome notion, of the erroneoufnefs of
which we are already fatisfied, then at
laft we are content to give it up with
out further ftruggle ; and then, and
not till then, our fatisfaction is compleat.

In the conceptions of the more confiderable part of thofe through whom
our religion has been handed down to
us, virtue, or rather godlinefs, which

was an improved fubftitute for virtue,
confifted in felf-denial : not in felf-denial for the fake of fociety, but of felf-
denial for its own fake.   One pretty
general rule ferved for moft occafions :
not to do what you had a mind to do ;
or, in other words, not to do what
would be for your advantage.   By
this of courfe was meant temporal advantage : to which fpiritual advantage
was underftood to be in conftant and
diametrical oppofition.   For, the proof
of a refolution, on the part of a being
of perfect power and benevolence, to
make his few favourites happy in a
ftate in which they *were to be*, was his
determined pleafure, that they fhould
keep

keep themfelves as much ftrangers to
happinefs as poffible, in a ftate in
which they *were*. Now to get money
is what moft men have a mind to do :
becaufe he who has money gets, as far
as it goes, moft other things that he
has a mind for. Of courfe nobody
was to get money: indeed why fhould
he, when he was not fo much as to
keep what he had got already? To
lend money at intereft, is to get money, or at leaft to try to get it: of
courfe it was a bad thing to lend money upon fuch terms. The better the
terms, the worfe it was to lend upon
them: but it was bad to lend upon
any terms, by which any thing could
be got. What made it much the worfe

G 3 was,

was, that it was acting like a Jew : for
though all Chriſtians at firſt were
Jews, and continued to do as Jews
did, after they had become Chriſtians,
yet, in procefs of time, it came to be
difcovered, that the diſtance between
the mother and the daughter church
could not be too wide.

By degrees, as old conceits gave
place to new, nature ſo far prevailed,
that the objections to getting money in
general, were pretty well over-ruled :
but ſtill this Jewiſh way of getting it,
was too odious to be endured. Chriſtians were too intent upon plaguing
Jews, to liſten to the fuggeſtion of
doing as Jews did, even though money

ney were to be got by it. Indeed the
eafier method, and a method pretty
much in vogue, was, to let the Jews
get the money any how they could,
and then fqueeze it out of them as it
was wanted.

In procefs of time, as queftions of
all forts came under difcuffion, and
this, not the leaft interefting, among
the reft, the anti-Jewifh fide of it found
no unopportune fupport in a paffage
of Ariftotle: that celebrated heathen,
who, in all matters wherein heathenifm
did not deftroy his competence, had
eftablifhed a defpotic empire over tne
Chriftian world. As fate would have
it, that great philofopher, with all his

in-

induftry, and all his penetration, not
withftanding the great number of
pieces of money that had paffed
through his hands (more perhaps
than over paffed through the hands
of philofopher before or fince), and
notwithftanding the uncommon pains
he had beftowed on the fubject of ge-
neration, had never been able to dif-
cover, in any one piece of money, any
organs for generating any other fuch
piece. Emboldened by fo ftrong a body
of negative proof, he ventured at laft
to ufher into the world the refult of his
obfervations, in the form of an univerfal propofition, that *all money is in its
nature barren.*   You, my friend, to
whofe caft of mind found reafon is
                                                much

much more congenial than antient phi-
lofophy, you have, I dare to fay, gone
before me in remarking, that the practical inference from this fhrewd obfervation, if it afforded any, fhould have
been, that it would be to no purpofe
for a man to try to get five per cent
out of money—not, that if he could
contrive to get fo much, there would
be any harm in it. But the fages of
thofe days did not view the matter in
that light.

A confideration that did not happen
to prefent itfelf to that great philofopher, but which had it happened to
prefent itfelf, might not have been
altogether unworthy of his notice, is,

G 5

that

that though a *daric* would not beget
another daric, any more than it would a
ram, or an ewe, yet for a daric which
a man borrowed, he might get a ram
and a couple of ewes, and that the
ewes, were the ram left with them a
certain time, would probably not be
barren. That then, at the end of the
year, he would find himfelf mafter of
his three fheep, together with two, if
not three, lambs ; and that, if he fold
his fheep again to pay back his daric,
and gave one of his lambs for the ufe
of it in the mean time, he would be
two lambs, or at leaft one lamb, richer,
than if he had made no fuch bargain.

Thefe

Thefe theological and philofophical conceits the offspring of the day, were not ill feconded by principles of a more permament complexion.

The bufinefs of a money lender, though only among Chriftians, and in Chriftian times, a profcribed profeffion, has no where, nor at any time, been a popular one. Thofe who have the re-folution to facrifice the prefent to future, are natural objects of envy to thofe who have facrificed the future to the prefent. The children who have eat their cake are the natural enemies of the children who have theirs. While the money is hoped for, and for a

fhort

ſhort time after it has been received,
he who lends it is a friend and benefactor : by the time the money is
ſpent, and the evil hour of reckoning
is come, the benefactor is found to
have changed his nature, and to have
put on the tyrant and the oppreſſor. It
is an oppreſſion for a man to reclaim his
own money : it is none to keep it from
him.   Among the inconſiderate, that
is among the great maſs of mankind,
ſelfiſh affections conſpire with the ſo-
cial in treaſuring up all favour for the
man of diſſipation, and in refuſing juſtice to the man of thrift who has ſup-
plied him.   In ſome ſhape or other that
favour attends the choſen object of it,
through

through every ftage of his career.
But, in no ftage of *his* career, can the
man of thrift come in for any fhare of
it. It is the general intereft of thofe
with whom a man lives, that his expence fhould be at leaft as great as his
circumftances will bear: becaufe there
are few expences which a man can
launch into, but what the benefit of
it is fhared, in fome proportion or
other, by thofe with whom he lives.
In that circle originates a ftanding
law, forbidding every man, on pain of
infamy, to confine his expences within
what is adjudged to be the meafure of
his means, faving always the power of
exceeding that limit, as much as he
thinks

thinks proper: and the means affigned
him by that law may be ever fo much
beyond his real means, but are fure
never to fall fhort of them. So clofe
is the combination thus formed between the idea of merit and the idea
of expenditure, that a difpofition to
fpend finds favour in the eyes even of
thofe who know that a man's circumftances do not entitle him to the means:
and an upftart, whofe chief recom—
mendation is this difpofition, fhall find
himfelf to have purchafed a permanent
fund of refpect, to the prejudice of the
very perfons at whofe expence he has
been gratifying his appetites and his
pride. The luftre, which the difplay
of

of borrowed wealth has diffufed over his chara&er, awes men, during the feafon of his profperity, into a fub-miffion to his infolence : and when the hand of adverfity has overtaken him at laft, the recolle&ion of the height, from which he is fallen, throws the veil of compaffion over his injuftice.

The condition of the man of thrift is the reverfe. His lafting opulence procures him a fhare, at leaft, of the fame envy, that attends the prodigal's tranfient difplay : but the ufe he makes of it procures him no part of the favour which attends the prodigal. In the fatisfa&ions he derives from that ufe, the pleafure of poffeffion, and the

idea

idea of enjoying, at fome diftant period, which may never arrive, nobody
comes in for any fhare.   In the midft
of his opulence he is regarded as a
kind of infolvent, who refufes to ho
nour the bills, which their rapacity
would draw upon him, and who is by
fo much the more criminal than other
infolvents, as not having the plea of in-
ability for an excufe.

Could there be any doubt of the dif-
favour, which attends the caufe of the
money-lender, in his competition with
the borrower, and of the difpofition of
the public judgment to facrifice the intereft of the former to that of the latter,

the

the ftage would afford a compendious
but a pretty concluſive proof of it. It
is the buſineſs of the dramatiſt to
ſtudy, and to conform to, the humours
and paſſions of thoſe, on the pleaſing
of whom he depends for his ſucceſs:
It is the courſe which reflection muſt
ſuggeſt to every man, and which a
man would naturally fall into, though
he were not to think about it. He
may, and very frequently does, make
magnificent pretences, of giving the
law to them: but woe be to him that
attempts to give them any other law
than what they are diſpoſed already to
receive. If he would attempt to lead
them

them one inch, it muſt be with great
caution,   and not without ſuffering
himſelf to be led by them at leaſt
a dozen.   Now, I queſtion, whether,
among all the inſtances in which a
borrower and a lender of money have
been brought together upon the ſtage,
from the days of Theſpis to the preſent, there ever was one, in which the
former was not recommended to favour in ſome ſhape or other, either to
admiration, or to love, or to pity, or
to all three ; and the other, the man of
thrift, conſigned to infamy.

Hence

Hence it is that, in reviewing and adjufting the interefts of thefe apparently rival parties, the advantage made by the borrower is fo apt to flip out of fight, and that made by the lender to appear in fo exaggerated a point of view. Hence it is, that though prejudice is fo far foftened, as to acquiefce in the lender's making fome advantage, left the borrower fhould lofe altogether the benefit of his affiftance, yet ftill the borrower is to have all the favour, and the lender's advantage is for ever to be clipped, and pared down, as low as it will bear. Firft it was to be confined to ten per cent.

then

then to eight, then to fix, then to five,
and now lately there was a report of
its being to be brought down to four;
with conftant liberty to fink as much
lower as it would.   The burthen of
thefe reftraints, of courfe, has been in-
tended exclufively for the lender: in
reality, as I think you have feen, it
preffes much more heavily upon the
borrower: I mean him who either becomes or in vain wifhes to become fo.
But the prefents directed by prejudice,
Dr. Smith will tell us, are not always
delivered according to their addrefs.
It was thus that the mill-ftone defign-
ed for the necks of thofe vermin, as
                                        they

they have been called, the dealers in corn, was found to fall upon the heads of the confumers. It is thus—but further exampies would lead me further from the purpofe.

LETTER

L E T T E R XI.

Compound Intereſt.

A Word or two I muſt trouble you with, concerning *compound intereſt* ; for compound intereſt is diſcountenanced by the law; I ſuppoſe, as a ſort of uſury. That, without an expreſs ſtipulation,

the

the law never gives it, I well remember :
whether, in cafe of an exprefs ftipula-
tion, the law allows it to be taken, I am
not abfolutely certain. I fhould fuppofe
it might : remembering covenants in
mortgages that intereft fhould become
principal. At any rate, I think the law
cannot well punifh it under the name of
ufury.

If the difcountenance fhewn to this
arrangement be grounded on the horror
of the fin of ufury, the impropriety of
fuch difcountenance follows of courfe,
from the arguments which fhew the un-
finfulnefs of that fin.

Other

Other argument againſt it, I believe, was never attempted, unleſs it were the giving to ſuch an arrangement the epithet of a *hard* one : in doing which, ſomething more like a reaſon is given, than one gets in ordinary from the common law.

If that conſiſtency were to be found in the common law, which has never yet been found in man's conduct, and which perhaps is hardly in man's nature, compound intereſt never could have been denied.

The

The views which fuggefted this denial, were, I dare to fay, very good :
the effects of it are, I am certain, very
pernicious.

If the borrower pays the intereft at
the day, if he performs his engagement,
that very engagement to which the law
pretends to oblige him to conform, the
lender, who receives that intereft, makes
compound intereft of courfe, by lending it out again, unlefs he choofes rather to expend it : he expects to receive
it at the day, or what meant the engagement? if he fails of receiving it, he is
by fo much a lofer. The borrower, by
paying it at the day, is no lofer : if he
does not pay it at the day, he is by

H   fo

fo much a gainer : a pain of difap-
pointment takes place inthe cafe of the
one, while no fuch pain takes place in
the cafe of the other. The caufe of
him whofe contention is to *catch a gain*,
is thus preferred to that of him whofe
contention is to avoid a lofs : contrary
to the reafonable and ufeful maxim of
that branch of the common law which
has acquired the name of equity. The
gain, which the law in its tendernefs thus
beftows on the defaulter, is an encour-
agement, a reward, which it holds out
for breach of faith, for iniquity, for in-
dolence, for negligence.

The

The lofs, which it thus throws upon the forbearing lender, is a punifhment which it inflicts on him for his forbearance: the power which it gives him of avoiding that lofs, by profecuting the borrower upon the inftant of failure, is thus converted into a reward which it holds out to him for his heard-heartednefs and rigour. Man is not quite fo good as it were to be wifhed he were; but he would be bad indeed, were he bad on all the occafions where the law, as far as depends on her, has made it his intereft fo to be.

It

It may be impoffible, fay you, it
often is impoffible, for the borrower to
pay the intereft at the day : and you
fay truly.   What is the inference ? That
the creditor fhould *not* have it in his
power to ruin the debtor for not paying
at the day, and that he *fhould* receive a
a compenfation for the lofs occafioned
by fuch failure.—He has it in his power
to ruin him, and he has it not in his
power to obtain fuch compenfation.
'The judge, were it poffible for an ar-
refted debtor to find his way into a
judge's chamber inftead of a fpunging.
houfe, might award a proper refpite,
fuited to the circumftances of the parties.

It

It is not poffible : but a refpite is purchafed, proper or not proper, perhaps
at ten times, perhaps at a hundred times
the expence of compound intereft, by
putting in bail, and fighting the creditor through all the windings of mifchievous and unneceffary delay. Of
the fatisfaction due either for the
original failure, or for the fubfequent
vexation by which it has been aggra-
vated, no part is ever received by the
injured creditor : but the inftruments
of the law receive, perhaps at his expence, perhaps at the debtor's, perhaps
ten times, perhaps a hundred times the
amount of that fatisfaction. Such is

H 3   the

the result of this tenderness of the law.

It is in consequence of such tenderness that on so many occasions a man, though ever so able, would find himself a loser by paying his just debts: those very debts of which the law has recognized the justice. The man who obeys the dictates of common honesty, the man who does what the law pretends to bid him, is wanting to himself. Hence your regular and securely profitable writs of error in the house of lords: hence your random and vindictive costs of one hundred pounds, and

two

two hundred pounds, now and then given in that houſe. It is natural, and it is ſomething, to find, in a company of lords, a zeal for juſtice : it is not natural, to find, in ſuch a company, a diſpoſition to bend down to the toil of calculation.

L E T-

———————

LETTER XII.

Maintenance and Champerty.

H AVING in the preceding letters had occaſion to lay down, and, as I flatter myſelf, to make good, the general principle, that *no man of ripe years, and of ſound mind, ought, out of loving-*

loving-kindnefs to him, to be hindered from making fuch a bargain, in the way of ob-taining money, as acting with his eyes open, he deems conducive to his intereft, I will take your leave for pufhing it a little farther, and extending the application of it to another clafs of regulations ftill lefs defenfible. I mean the antique laws againft what are called Mainte-nance and Champerty.

To the head of *Maintenance,* I think you refer, befides other offences which are to the prefent purpofe, that of pur-chafing, upon any terms, any claim, which it requires a fuit at law, or in equity, to enforce.

H 5   Champerty,

Champerty, which is but a particular modification of this fin of Maintenance, is, I think, the furnifhing a man who has fuch a claim, with regard to a real eftate, fuch money as he may have occafion for, to carry on fuch claim, upon the terms of receiving a part of the eftate in cafe of fuccefs.

What the penalties are for thefe offences I do not recollect, nor do I think it worth while hunting for them, though I have Blackftone at my elbow. They are, at any rate, fufficiently fevere to anfwer the purpofe, the rather as the bargain is made void.

To

To illuftrate the mifchievoufnefs of the laws by which they have been created, give me leave to tell you a ftory, which is but too true an one, and which happened to fall within my own obfervation.

A gentleman of my acquaintance had fucceeded, during his minority, to an eftate of about 3000l. a year; I won't fay where. His guardian, concealing from him the value of the eftate, which circumftances rendered it eafy for him to do, got a conveyance of it from him, during his nonage, for a trifle. Immediately upon the ward's coming of age, the guardian, keeping him ftill in darknefs, found

means

means to get the conveyance confirmed. Some years afterwards, the ward
difcovered the value of the inheritance
he had been throwing away. Private
reprefentations proving, as it may be
imagined, ineffectual, he applied to a
court of equity. The fuit was in fome
forwardnefs: the opinion of the ableft
counfel highly encouraging: but money
there remained none. We all know
but too well, that, in fpite of the un-
impeachable integrity of the bench,
that branch of juftice, which is particularly dignified with the name of
equity, is only for thofe who can afford
to throw away one fortune for the
chance of recovering another. Two
perfons, however, were found, who, between

tween them, were content to defray the
expence of the ticket for this lottery,
on condition of receiving half the
prize. The profpect now became encouraging: when unfortunately one of
the adventurers, in exploring the re-
ceffes of the bottomlefs pit, happened to
dig up one of the old ftatutes againft
Champerty. This blew up the whole
project : however the defendant, un-
derftanding that, fome how or other,
his antagonift had found fupport, had
thought fit in the mean time to propofe
terms, which the plaintiff, after his
fupport had thus dropped from under
him, was very glad to clofe with.
He received, I think it was, 3000l.:
and

and for that he gave up the eftate,
which was worth about as much year-
ly, together with the arrears, which
were worth about as much as the
eftate.

Whether, in the barbarous age
which gave birth to thefe barbarous
precautions, whether, even under the
zenith of feudal anarchy, fuch fetter-
ing regulations could have had reafon
on their fide, is a queftion of curiofity
rather than ufe. My notion is, that
there never was a time, that there never could have been, or can be a time,
when the pufhing of fuitors away from
court with one hand, while they are
beckoned into it with another, would
not

not be a policy equally faithlefs, in-
confiftent, and abfurd. But, what
every body muft acknowledge, is,
that, to the times which called forth
thefe laws, and in which alone they
could have ftarted up, the prefent are
as oppofite as light to darknefs. A
mifchief, in thofe times, it feems, but
too common, though a mifchief not to
be cured by fuch laws, was, that a
man would buy a weak claim, in
hopes that power might convert it
into a ftrong one, and that the fword
of a baron, ftalking into court with a
rabble of retainers at his heels, might
ftrike terror into the eyes of a judge
upon the bench. At prefent, what
cares

cares an Englifh judge for the fwords
of an hundred barons? Neither fear-
ing nor hoping, hating nor loving, the
judge of our days is ready with equal
phlegm to adminifter, upon all occafions, that fyftem, whatever it be, of
juftice, or injuftice, which the law has
put into his hands. A difpofition fo
confonant to duty could not have then
been hoped for: one more confonant
is hardly to be wifhed. Wealth has
indeed the monopoly of juftice againft
poverty: and fuch monopoly it is the
direct tendency and neceffary effect of
regulations like thefe to ftrengthen and
confirm. But with this monopoly no
judge that lives now is at all chargeable.
                                                        The

The law created this monopoly: the law, whenever it pleafes, may diffolve it.

I will not however fo far wander from my fubject as to enquire what meafure might have been neceffary to afford a full relief to the cafe of that unfortunate gentleman, any more than to the cafes of fo many other gentlemen who might be found, as unfortunate as he. I will not infift upon fo ftrange and fo inconceivable an arrangement, as that of the judge's feeing both parties face to face in the fiift inftance, obferving what the facts are in difpute, and declaring, that as the facts fhould turn out this way or that

way,

way, fuch or fuch would be his decree.
At prefent, I confine myfelf to the
removal of fuch part of the mifchief, as
may arife from the general conceit of
keeping men out of difficulties, by
cutting them off from fuch means of
relief as each man's fituation may afford. A fpunge in this, as in fo many
other cafes, is the only needful, and
only availing remedy : one ftroke of it
for the mufty laws againft maintenance
and champerty : another for the more
recent ones againft ufury. Confider,
for example, what would have refpec-
tively been the effect of two fuch
ftrokes, in the cafe of the unfortunate
gentleman I have been fpeaking of.

By

By the firſt, if what is called equity
has any claim to confidence, he would
have got, even after paying of his
champerty-uſurers, 1500 l. a year in
land, and about as much in money:
inſtead of getting, and that only by an
accident, 3000 l. once told. By the
other, there is no ſaying to what a degree he might have been benefited.
May I be allowed to ſtretch ſo far in
favour of the law as to ſuppoſe, that ſo
ſmall a ſum as 500 l. would have car-
ried him through his ſuit, in the courſe
of about three years? I am ſenſible,
that may be thought but a ſhort ſum,
and this but a ſhort term, for a ſuit in
equity: but, for the purpoſe of illuſ-
tration,

tration, it may ferve as well as a longer.
Suppofe he had fought this neceffary
fum in the way of borrowing ; and had
been fo fortunate, or, as the laws
againft the fin of ufury would ftile it,
fo unfortunate, as to get it at 200 per
cent. He would then have purchafed
his 6000 l, a year at the price of half as
much once paid, viz. 3000 l. ; inftead
of felling it at that price. Whether, if
no fuch laws againft ufury had been in
being, he could have got the money,
even at that rate, I will not pretend to
fay : perhaps he might not have got it
under ten times that rate, perhaps he
might have got it at the tenth part of
that rate. Thus far, I think, we may

fay,

fay, that he might, and probably
would, have been the better for the re-
peal of thofe laws: but thus far we
muſt fay, that it is impoſſible he ſhould
have been the worſe. The terms, upon which he met with adventurers
willing to relieve him, though they
come not within that ſcanty field,
which the law, in the narrownefs of its
views, calls ufury, do, in the prefent
cafe at twenty years purchafe of the
3000l. a year he was content to have
facrificed for fuch affiſtance, amount,
in effect, to 4000 per cent. Whether
it was likely that any man, who was
difpofed to venture his money, at all,
upon fuch a chance, would have
                                        thought

thought of infifting upon fuch a rate
of intereft, I will leave you to imagine : but thus much may be faid with
confidence, becaufe the fact demon-
ftrates it, that at a rate not exceeding
this, the fum would actually have been
fupplied. Whatever becomes then of
the laws againft maintenance and
champerty, the example in queftion,
when applied to the laws againft ufury, ought, I think, to be fufficient to
convince us, that fo long as the expence of feeking relief at law ftands on
its prefent footing, the purpofe of feeking that relief will, of itfelf, independently of every other, afford a fufficient
ground for allowing any man, or eve-

ry

ry man, to borrow money on any
terms he can obtain it.

Crichoff,
in White Ruſſia,
March 1787.

LETTER

L E T T E R XIII.

To Dr. Smith, on Projects in Arts, &c.

SIR,

I Forget what fon of controverfy it
was, among the Greeks, who having
put himfelf to fchool, to a profeffor
of eminence, to learn what, in thofe
days,

days, went by the name of wifdom,
chofe an attack upon his mafter for
the firft public fpecimen of his profi-
ciency. This fpecimen, whatever en-
tertainment it might have afforded to
the audience, afforded, it may be fuppofed, no great fatisfaction to the mafter: for the thefis was, that the pupil
owed him nothing for his pains. For
my part, being about to fhew myfelf
in one refpect as ungrateful as the
Greek, it may be a matter of prudence
for me to look out for fomething like
candour by way of covering to my in-
gratitude: inftead therefore of pretending to owe you nothing, I fhall
begin with acknowledging, that, as far

I   as

as your track coincides with mine, I
fhould come much nearer the truth,
were I to fay I owed you every thing.
Should it be my fortune to gain any
advantage over you, it muft be with
weapons which you have taught me to
wield, and with which you yourfelf
have furnifhed me : for, as all the great
ftandards of truth, which can be ap-
pealed to in this line, owe, as far as I
can underftand, their eftablifhment to
you, I can fee fcarce any other way of
convicting you of any error or over-
fight, than by judging you out of your
own mouth.

In

In the feries of letters to which this will form a fequel, I had travelled nearly thus fa. in my refearches into the policy of the laws fixing the rate of intereft, combating fuch arguments as fancy rather than obfervation had fuggefted to my views, when, on a fudden, recollection prefented me with your formidable image, beftriding the ground over which I was travelling pretty much at my eafe. and oppofing the fhield of your authority to any arguments I could produce.

It was a reflection mentioned by Cicero as affording him fome comfort, that the employment his talents till

that

that time had met with, had been
chiefly on the defending fide. How
little foever bleft, on any occafion, with
any portion of his eloquence, I may,
on the prefent occafion, however, indulge myfelf with a portion of what
conftituted his comfort : for, if I pre-
fume to contend with you, it is only
in defence of what I look upon as, not
only an innocent, but a moft meritorious race of men, who are fo unfortunate as to have fallen under the rod of
your difpleafure. I mean *projectors :*
under which invidious name I underftand you to comprehend, in particular,
all fuch perfons as, in the purfuit of
wealth, ftrike out into any new channel,

nel, and more efpecially into any channel of invention.

It is with the profeffed view of
checking, or rather of crufhing, thefe
adventurous fpirits, whom you rank
with " prodigals," that you approve
of the laws which limit the rate of intereft, grounding yourfelf on the tendency, they appear to you to have, to
keep the capital of the country out of
two fuch different fets of hands.

The paffage, I am fpeaking of, is
in the fourth chapter of your fecond
book, volume the fecond of the 8vo
edition of 1784. " The legal rate"

I 3   (you

(you fay) " it is to be obferved, though
" it ought to be fomewhat above,
" ought not to be much above, the
" loweft market rate.   If the legal rate
" of intereft in Great Britain, for exam-
" ple, was fixed fo high as eight or ten
" per cent. the greater part of the mo-
" ney which was to be lent, would be
" lent to prodigals and projectors, who
" alone would be willing to give this
" high intereft.   Sober people, who
" will give for the ufe of money no
" more than a part of what they are
" likely to make by the ufe of it,
" would not venture into the compe-
" tition.   A great part of the capital
" of the country would thus be kept
                              " out

" out of the hands which were moſt
" likely to make a profitable and ad-
" vantageous uſe of it, and thrown
" into thoſe which were moſt likely to
" waſte and deſtroy it.   Where the
" legal intereſt on the contrary, is
" fixed but a very little above the
" loweſt market rate, ſober people are
" univerſally preferred as borrowers,
" to prodigals and projectors.   The
" perſon who lends money, gets nearly
" as much intereſt from the former, as
" he dares to take from the latter,
" and his money is much ſafer in the
" hands of the one ſet of people than
" in thoſe of the other.   A great part
" of the capital of the country is thus
                              " thrown

" thrown into the hands in which it
" is moſt likely to be employed with
" advantage."

It happens fortunately for the ſide
you appear to have taken, and as unfortunately for mine, that the appella-
tive, which the cuſtom of the language
has authorized you, and which the poverty and perverſity of the language
has in a manner forced you to make
uſe of, is one, which, along with the
idea of the ſort of perſons in queſtion,
conveys the idea of reprobation, as in-
diſcriminately and deſervedly applied
to them. With what juſtice or conſiſtency, or by the influence of what
cauſes,

caufes, this ftamp of indifcriminate reprobation has been thus affixed, it is
not immediately neceffary to enquire.
But, that it does ftand thus affixed, you
and every body elfe, I imagine, will be
ready enough to allow. This being
the cafe, the queftion ftands already
decided, in the firft inftance at leaft,
if not irrevocably, in the judgments of
all thofe, who, unable or unwilling to
be at the pains of analyfing their ideas,
fuffer their minds to be led captive by
the tyranny of founds : that is, I
doubt, of by far the greater proportion of thofe whom we are likely to
have to judge us. In the conceptions
of all fuch perfons, to afk whether it

I 5   be

be fit to reftrain projects, and projectors, will be as much as to afk, whether it be fit to reftrain rafhnefs, and
folly, and abfurdity, and knavery, and
wafte.

Of prodigals I fhall fay no more at
prefent. I have already ftated my reafons for thinking, that it is not among
them that we are to look for the natural cuftomers for money at high rates
of intereft.   As far as thofe reafons
are conclufive, it will follow, that, of
the two forts of men you mention as
proper objects of the burthen of thefe
reftraints, prodigals and projectors,
that burthen falls exclufively on the
latter.

latter. As to thefe, what your definition is of projectors, and what defcriptions of perfons you meant to include under the cenfure conveyed by that name, might be material for the purpofe of judging of the propriety of that cenfure, but makes no difference in judging of the propriety of the law, which that cenfure is employed to juftify. Whether you yourfelf, were the feveral claffes of perfons made to pafs before you in review, would be difpofed to pick out this or that clafs, or this and that individual, in order to exempt them from fuch cenfure, is what for that purpofe we have no need to enquire. The law, it is

certain,

certain, makes no fuch diftinctions, it
falls with equal weight, and with all
its weight, upon all thofe perfons,
without diftinction, to whom the term
projectors, in the moft unpartial and
extenfive fignification of which it is
capable, can be applied.   It falls at
any rate (to repeat fome of the words
of my former definition), upon all
fuch perfons, as, in the purfuit of
wealth, or even of any other object, endeavour, by the affiftance of
wealth, to ftrike into any channel of
invention.   It falls upon all fuch perfons, as, in the cultivation of any of
thofe arts which have been by way of
eminence termed *ufeful*, direct their endeavours

deavours to any of thofe departments in which their utility fhines moft confpicuous and indubitable ; upon all fuch perfons as, in the line of any of their purfuits, aim at any thing that can be called *improvement* ; whether it confift in the production of any new article adapted to man's ufe, or in the meliorating the quality, or diminifhing the expence, of any of thofe which are already known to us. It falls, in fhort, upon every application of the human powers, in which ingenuity ftands in need of wealth for its affiftant.

High

High and extraordinary rates of in
tereſt, how little ſoever adapted to the
ſituation of the prodigal, are certainly,
as you very juſtly obſerve, particularly
adapted to the ſituation of the projector: nor however to that of the im-
prudent projector only, nor even to
his caſe more than another's, but to
that of the prudent and well-grounded
projector, if the exiſtence of ſuch a
being were to be ſuppoſed. Whatever
be the prudence or other qualities of
the project, in whatever circumſtance
the novelty of it may lie, it has this
ci cumſtance againſt it, viz that it is
new   But the rates of intereſt, the
higheſt rates allowed, are, as you ex-
                                     preſsly

prefsly fay they are, and as you would
have them to be, adjufted to the fituation which the fort of trader is in,
whofe tradelruns in the old channels,
and to the beft fecurity which fuch
channels can afford. But, in the nature of things, no new trade, no trade
carried on in any new channel, can afford a fecurity equal to that which
may be afforded by a trade carried
on in any of the old ones : in whatever
light the matter might appear to perfect intelligence, in the eye of every
prudent perfon, exerting the beft powers of judging which the fallible condition of the human faculties affords,
the novelty of any commercial adventure

ture will oppofe a chance of ill fuccefs, fuperadded to every one which could attend the fame, or any other adventure, already tried, and proved to be profitable by experience.

The limitation of the profit that is to be made, by lending money to perfons embarked in trade, will render the monied man more anxious, you may fay, about the goodnefs of his fecurity and accordingly more anxious to fatisfy himfelf refpecting the prudence of a project, in the carrying on of which the money is to be employed, than he would be otherwife : and in this way it may be thought that thefe
laws

laws *have* a tendency to pick out the good projects from the bad, and favour the former at the expence of the latter. The first of thefe pofitions I admit : but I can never admit the confequence to follow. A prudent man, (I mean nothing more than a man of ordinary prudence) a prudent man acting under the fole governance of prudential motives, I ftill fay will not, in thefe circumftances, pick out the good projects from the bad, for he will not meddle with projects at all. He will pick out old-eftablifhed trades from all forts of projects, good and bad ; for with a new project, be it ever fo promifing, he never will have any thing

thing to do. By every man that has money, five per cent. or whatever be the higheft legal rate, is at all times, and always will be, to be had upon the very beft fecurity, that the beft and moft profperous old-eftablifhed trade can-afford. Traders in general, I be-lieve, it is commonly underftood, are well enougu inclined to enlarge their capital, as far as all the money they can borrow at the higheft legal rate, while that rate is fo low as 5 per cent. will enlarge it. How it is pof-fible therefore for a projeﬔ, be it ever fo promifing, to afford, to a lender at any fuch rate of intereft, terms equally advantageous, upon the whole, with thofe

thofe he might be fure of obtaining
from an old-eftablifhed bufinefs, is more
than I can conceive. Loans of money may certainly chance, now and
then, to find their way into the pockets of projectors as well as of other
men : but when this happens it muft
be through incautioufnefs, or friendfhip, or the expectation of fome colla-
teral benefit, and not through any idea
of the advantageoufnefs of the tranfaction, in the light of a pecuniary bargain.

I fhould

I fhould not expect to fee it alledged,
that there is any thing, that fhould render the number of well-grounded projects, in comparifon of the ill-grounded,
lefs in time future, than it has been in
time paft. I am fure at leaft that I
know of no reafons why it fhould be
fo, though I know of fome reafons,
which I fhall beg leave to fubmit to
you by and by, which appear to me
pretty good ones, why the advantage
fhould be on the fide of futurity. But,
unlefs the ftock of well-grounded projects is already fpent, and the whole
ftock of ill-grounded projects that
ever were poffible, are to be looked
for exclufively in the time to come,
the

the cenfure you have paffed on projectors, meafuring ftill the extent of it by
that of the operation of the laws in the
defence of which it is employed, looks
as far backward as forward : it con-
demns as rafh and ill-grounded, all
thofe projects, by which our fpecies
have been fucceffively advanced from
that ftate in which acorns were their
food, and raw hides their cloathing,
to the ftate in which it ftands at prefent: for think, Sir, let me beg of you,
whether whatever is now the *routine*
of trade was not, at its commence-
ment, *project ?* whether whatever is
now *eftablifhment*, was not, at one time,
innovation ?

How

How it is that the tribe of well-grounded projects, and of prudent projectors (if by this time I may have your leave for applying this epithet to some at leaft among the projectors of time paft), have managed to ftruggle through the obftacles which the laws in queftion have been holding· in their way, it is neither eafy to know, nor neceffary to enquire. Manifeft enough, I think ; it muft be by this time, that difficulties, and thofe not inconfiderable ones, thofe laws muft have been holding, in the way of projects of all forts of improvement (if I may fay fo) in every line, fo long as they have had exiftence : reafonable therefore it muft

be

be to conclude, that, had it not been for thefe difcouragements, projects of all forts, well-grounded and fuccefsful ones, as well as others, would have been more numerous than they have been : and that accordingly, on the other hand, as foon, if ever, as thefe difcourage-ments fhall be removed, projects of all forts, and among the reft, well-ground-ed and fuccefsful ones, will be more numerous than they would otherwife have been : in fhort, that, as, without thefe difcouragements, the progrefs of mankind, in the career of profperity, would have been greater than it has been under them in time paft, fo, were they to be removed, it would be

at

at leaft proportionably greater in time
future.

That I have done you no injuftice,
in affigning to your idea of projectors
fo great a latitude, and that the unfavourable opinion you have profeffed
to entertain of them is not confined to
the above paffage, might be made, I
think, pretty apparent, if it be material, by another paffage in the tenth
chapter of your firft book*. " The
" eftablifhment of any new manufac-
" ture, of any new branch of com-
" merce, or of any new practice in

---

* Edit. 1784, 8vo. p. 177.

agri-

" agriculture," all thefe you comprehend by name under the lift of " *pro-
jeĉts* :" of every one of them you obferve, that " it is a fpeculation from
" which the *projeĉtor* promifes himfelf
" extraordinary profits. Thefe pro-
" fits (you add) are fometimes *very*
" *great,* and fometimes, *more frequently*
" *perhaps,* they are *quite otherwife :* but
" in general they bear no regular pro-
" portion to thofe of other old trades
" in the neighbourhood. If the pro-
" jeĉt fucceeds, they are commonly
" at firft very high. When the trade
" or praĉtice becomes thoroughly efta-
" blifhed and well known, the com-
" petition reduces them to the level of

K   " other

" other trades." But on this head
I forbear to infift : nor fhould I
have taken this liberty of giving you
back your own words, but in the
hope of feeing fome alteration made
in them in your next edition, fhould I
be fortunate enough to find my fentiments confirmed by your's. In other
refpects, what is effential to the pub-
lick, is, what the error is in the fentiments entertained, not who it is that en-
tertains them.

I know not whether the obfervations which I have been troubling you
with, will be thought to need, or whether they will be thought to receive,
any additional fupport from thofe
                                    com-

comfortable pofitions, of which you have made fuch good and fuch fre-quent ufe, concerning the conftant ten-dency of mankind to get forward in the career of profperity, the prevalence of prudence over imprudence, in the fum of private conduct at leaft, and the fuperior fitnefs of individuals for managing their own pecuniary con-cerns, of which they know the par-ticulars and the circumftances, in com-parifon of the legiflator, who can have no fuch knowledge. I will make the experiment : for, fo long as I have the mortification to fee you on the oppo-fite fide, I can never think the ground I have taken ftrong enough, while any thing remains that appears capable of rendering it ftill ftronger.

K 2 " With

" With regard to mifconduct, the
" number of prudent and fuccefsful un-
" dertakings" (you obferve*) " is every
" where much greater than that of in-
" judicious and unfuccefsful ones.
" After all our complaints of the fre-
" quency of bankruptcies, the unhap-
" py men who fall into this misfor-
" tune make but a very fmall part of
" the whole number engaged in trade,
" and all other forts of bufinefs ; not
" much more perhaps than one in a
" thoufand."

'Tis in fupport of this pofition that
you appeal to hiftory for the conftant
and uninterrupted progrefs of mankind,

* B. II ch. iii. edit. 8vo 1784, vol. ii. p. 20.

in

in our ifland at leaft, in the career of
profperity : calling upon any one who
fhould entertain a doubt of the fact, to
divide the hiftory into any number of
periods, from the time of Cæfar's vifit
down to the prefent : propofing for
inftance the refpective æras of the Re-
ftoration, the Acceffion of Elizabeth,
that of Henry VII. the Norman Con-
queft, and the Heptarchy, and putting
it to the fceptic to find out, if he can,
among all thefe periods, any one at
which the condition of the country was
not more profperous than at the period
immediately preceding it ; fpite of fo
many wars, and fires, and plagues,
and all other public calamities, with

K 3   which

which it has been at different times af-
flicted, whether by the hand of God,
or by the misconduct of the sovereign.
No very easy task, I believe : the fact
is too manifest for the most jaundiced
eye to escape seeing it :—But what
and whom we are to thank for it, but
projects, and projectors ?

 " No," I think I hear you saying,
" I will not thank projectors for it, I
" will rather thank the laws, which by
" fixing the rates of interest have
" been exercising their vigilance in
" repressing the temerity of projectors,
" and preventing their imprudence
" from making those defalcations from
" the sum of national prosperity which
                                   " it

" it would not have failed to make
" had it been left free. If, during all
" thefe periods, that adventurous race
" of men had been left at liberty by
" the laws to give full fcope to their
" rafh enterprizes, the increafe of na-
" tional profperity during thefe periods
" might have afforded fome ground
" for regarding them in a more favour-
" able point of view. But the fact is,
" that their activity has had thefe laws
" to check it ; without which checks
" you muft give me leave to fuppofe,
" that the current of profperity if not
" totally ftopt, or turned the other
" way, would at any rate have been
" more or lefs retarded. Here then"
" (you conclude) " lies the difference
be-

" between us : what you look upon
" as the caufe of the increafe about
" which we are both agreed, I look
" upon as an obftacle to it : and what
" you look upon as the obftacle, I look
" upon as the caufe."

Inftead of ftating this as a fort of
plea that might be urged by you, I
ought, perhaps, rather to have mentioned it as what might be urged by
fome people in your place : for as I do
not imagine your penetration would
fuffer you to reft fatisfied with it, ftill
lefs can I fuppofe that, if you were
not, your candour would allow you to
make ufe of it as if you were.

To prevent your refting fatisfied with
it, the following confiderations would I
think be fufficient.

In the firſt place, of the ſeven periods which you have pitched upon,
as ſo many ſtages for the eye to reſt
at in viewing the progreſs of proſpe-
rity, it is only during the three laſt,
that the country has had the benefit,
if ſuch we are to call it, of theſe laws :
for it is to the reign of Henry VIII. that
we owe the firſt of them.

Here a multitude of queſtions might
be ſtarted : Whether the curbing of
projectors formed any part of the de-
ſign of that firſt ſtatute, or whether
the views of it were not wholly confined to the reducing the gains of that
obnoxious and envied claſs of men,
the money-lenders ? Whether projectors
have been moſt abundant before that

K 5   ſtatute,

ftatute, or fince that ftatute ? And
whether the nation has fuffered as you
might fay—benefited, as I fhould fay,
moft by them, upon the whole, during the former period or the latter ?
All thefe difcuffions, and many more
that might be ftarted, I decline engag-
ing in, as more likely to retard, than to
forward, our coming to any agreement
concerning the main queftion.

In the next place, I muft here take
the liberty of referring you to the
proof, which I think I have already
given, of the propofition, that the reftraints in queftion could never have
had the effect, in any degree of leffening the proportion of bad projects to
good ones, but only of diminifhing,

as

as far as their influence may have extended, the total number of projects, good and bad together. Whatever therefore was the general tendency of the projecting fpirit previoufly to the firft of thefe laws, fuch it muft have remained ever fince, for any effect which they could have had in purifying and correcting it.

But what may appear more fatisfactory perhaps than both the above confiderations, and may afford us the beft help towards extricating ourfelves from the perplexity, which the plea I have been combating (and which I thought it neceffary to bring to view, as the beft that could be urged) feems much better calculated to plunge us into,
than

than bring us out of, is, the confideration of the fmall effect which the
greateft wafte that can be conceived to
have been made within any compafs of
time, by injudicious projects, can have
had on the fum of profperity, even in
the eftimation of thofe whofe opinion
is moft unfavourable to projectors, in
comparifon of the effect which within
the fame compafs of time muft have
been produced by *prodigality*.

Of the two caufes, and only two
caufes, which you mention, as contri-
buting to retard the accumulation of
national wealth, as far as the conduct
of individuals is concerned, projecting,
as I obferved before, is the one, and

prodi-

prodigality is the other : but the de-
triment, which fociety can receive even
from the concurrent efficacy of both
thefe caufes, you reprefent, on feveral occafions, as inconfiderable ; and,
if I do not mifapprehend you, too
inconfiderable, either to need, or to
warrant, the interpofition of government to oppofe it. Be this as it may
with regard to projecting and prodigality taken together, with regard to
prodigality at leaft, I am certain I
do not mifapprehend you. On this
fubject you ride triumphant, and chaf-
tife the " impertinence and prefump-
" tion of kings and minifters," with
a tone of authority, which it required
a courage like yours to venture upon,
and a genius like your's to warrant a
man

man to affume*.   After drawing the
parallel between private thrift and public profufion.   " It is" (you conclude)
" the higheft impertinence and pre-
" fumption therefore in kings and mi-
" nifters *to pretend to watch over the eco-*
" *nomy of private people* and to reftrain
" their expence, either by fumptuary
" laws, or by prohibiting the importa-
" tion of foreign luxuries.   They are
" themfelves always, and without ex-
" ception the greateft fpendthrifts in the
" fociety.   Let them look well after
" their own expence, and they may
" fafely truft private people with theirs.
" If their own extravagance does not

* B. II. ch. iii. vol. ii. p. 27. edit. 8vo.
1784.

" ruin

" ruin the ftate, that of their fubjects
" never will."

That the employing the expedients
you mention for reftraining prodigality, is indeed generally, perhaps even
without exception, improper, and in
many cafes even ridiculous, I agree
with you ; nor will I here ftep afide,
from my fubject to defend from that
imputation another mode fuggefted in
a former part of thefe papers. But
however prefumptious and impertinent it may be for the fovereign to attempt in any way to check by legal
reftraints the *prodigality* of individuals,
to attempt to check their *bad manage-
ment* by fuch reftraints feems abun-
dantly

dantly more fo. To err in the way of
prodigality is the lot, though, as you
well obferve, not of *many* men, in
comparifon of the whole mafs of mankind, yet at leaft of *any* man : the ftuff
fit to make a prodigal of is to be found
in every alehoufe, and under every
hedge. But even to *err* in the way of
projecting is the lot only of the privi-
leged few. Prodigality, though not
fo common as to make any very material drain ·from the general mafs of
wealth, is however too common to be
regarded as a mark of diftinction or
as a fingularity. But the ftepping
afide from any of the beaten paths of
traffic, *is* regarded as a fingularity, as
ferving to diftinguifh a man from other
men.

men. Even where it requires no genius, no peculiarity of talent, as where
it confifts in nothing more than the
finding out a new market to buy or
fell in, it requires however at leaft a
degree of courage, which is not to be
found in the common herd of men.
What fhall we fay of it, where, in addition to the vulgar quality of courage, it requires the rare endowment
of genius, as in the inftance of all thofe
fucceffive enterprizes by which arts
and manufactures have been brought
from their original nothing to their
prefent fplendor ? Think how fmall
a part of the community thefe muft
make, in comparifon of the race of
prodigals ; of that very race, which,

were

were it only on account of the fmall-
nefs of its number, would appear too
inconfiderable to you to deferve attention. Yet prodigality is effentially
and neceffarily hurtful, as far as it goes,
to the opulence of the ftate : projecting, only by accident. Every prodigal without exception, impairs, by the
very fuppofition impairs, if he does
not annihilate, his fortune. But it
certainly is not every projector that
impairs his : it is not every projector
that would have done fo, had there
been none of thofe wife laws to hinder him : for the fabric of national
opulence, that fabric of which you pro-
claim, with fo generous an exultation,
the continual increafe, that fabric, in
every

every apartment of which, innumera-
ble as they are, it required the repro-
bated hand of a projector to lay the firſt
ſtone, has required ſome hands at leaſt
to be employed, and that ſucceſsfully
employed. When in compariſon of
the number of prodigals, which is too
inconſiderable to deſerve notice, the
number of projectors of all kinds is ſo
much more inconſiderable— and when
from this inconſiderable number, muſt
be deducted, the not inconſiderable proportion of ſucceſsful projectors—and
from this remainder again, all thoſe who
can carry on their projects without need
of borrowing—think whether it is poſſi-
ble, that this laſt remainder could afford
a multitude, the reducing of which would
be

be an object, deferving the interpofition of government by its magnitude, even taking for granted that it were an object proper in its nature ?

If it be ftill a queftion, whether it be worth while for government, by its *rea-fon*, to attempt to controul the conduct of men vifibly and undeniably under the dominion of *paffion*, and acting, under that dominion, contrary to the dictates of their own reafon : in fhort, to effect what is acknowledged to be their better judgment, againft what every body, even themfelves, would acknowledge to be their worfe ; is it endurable that the legiflator fhould by violence fubftitute his own pretended reafon, the refult of a momentary and fcornful glance,

glance, the offspring of wantonnefs and arrogance, much rather than of focial anxiety and ftudy, in the place of the humble reafon of individuals, binding itfelf with all its force to that very ob-ject which he pretends to have in view? Nor let it be forgotten, that, on the fide of the individual in this ftrange compe-tition, there is the moft perfect and mi-nute knowledge and information, which intereft, the whole intereft of a man's re-putation and fortune, can enfure : on the fide of the legiflator, the moft perfect ignorance. All that he knows, all that he can know, is, that the enterprize is a *project*, which, merely becaufe it is fuf-ceptible of that obnoxious name, he looks upon as a fort of cock; for him, in child-

ifh

ifh wantonnefs, to fhy at.—Shall the
blind lead the blind ? is a queftion that
has been put of old to indicate the height
of folly : but what then fhall we fay of
him who, being neceffarily blind, infifts
on leading, in paths he never trod in,
thofe who can fee ?

It muft be by fome diftinction too
fine for my conception, if you clear
yourfelf from the having taken, on another occafion, but on the very point in
queftion, the fide, on which it would be
my ambition to fee you fix.

" What is the fpecies of domeftic in-
" duftry which his capital can employ,
" and of which the produce is likely to
" be of the greateft value, every indi-
               " vidual"

" vidual" (you fay*), " it is evident,
" can, in his local fituation, judge much
" better than any ftatefman or lawgiv-
" er can do for him. The ftatefman,
" who fhould attempt to direct private
" people in what manner they ought to
" employ their capitals, would not only
" load himfelf with a moft unneceffary
" attention, but affume an authority
" which could fafely be trufted, not only
" to no fingle perfon, but to no counfel
" or fenate whatfoever, and which would
" no where be fo dangerous as in the
" hands of a man who had folly and pre-
" fumption enough to fancy himfelf fit
" to exercife it.

" To give the monopoly of the home
" market to the produce of domeftic in-
" duftry

" duſtry, in any particular art or ma-
" nufacture, is in ſome meaſure to di-
" rect private people in what manner
" they ought to employ their capitals,
" and muſt in almoſt all caſes be either
" a uſeleſs or a hurtful regulation."—
Thus far you : and I add, to limit the
legal intereſt to a rate at which the car-
riers on of the oldeſt and beſt-eſtabliſhed
and leaſt hazardous trades are always
glad to borrow, is to give the monopoly
of the money market to thoſe traders,
as againſt the projectors of new imagined trades, not one of which but, were
it only from the circumſtances of its novelty, muſt, as I have already obſerved,
appear more hazardous than the old.

Theſe,

Thefe, in comparifon, are but incon-
clufive topics. I touched upon them
merely as affording, what appeared to
me the only fhadow of a plea, that could
be brought, in defence of the policy I
am contending againft, I come back
therefore to my firft ground, and beg
you once more to confider, whether, of
all that hoft of manufactures, which we
both exult in as the caufes and ingredi-
ents of national profperity, there be a
fingle one, that could have exifted at firft
but in the fhape of a project. But, if
a regulation, the tendency and effect of
which is merely to check projects, in as
far as they are projects, without any fort
of tendency, as I have fhewn, to weed
out the bad ones, is defenfible in its pre-

L   fent

fent ſtate of imperfect efficacy, it ſhould
not only have been defenſible, but much
more worthy of our approbation, could
the efficacy of it have been ſo far
ſtrengthened and compleated as to have
oppoſed, from the beginning, an unſur-
mountable bar to all ſorts of projects
whatſoever : that is to ſay, if ſtretch-
ing forth its hand over the rudiments of
ſociety, it had confined us, from the
beginning, to mud for our habitations,
to ſkins for our cloathing, and to acorns
for our food.

I hope you may by this time be diſpoſed to allow me, that we have not
been ill ſerved by the projects of time
paſt. I have already intimated, that I
could not ſee any reaſon why we ſhould
　　　　　　　　　　　appre-

apprehend our being worfe ferved by the projeɕts of time future. I will now venture to add, that I think I do fee reafon, why we fhould expeɕt to be ſtill better and better ferved by thefe pro-jeɕts, than by thofe. I mean better upon the whole, in virtue of the reduc-tion which experience, if experience be worth any thing, fhould make in the proportion of the number of the ill-grounded and unfuccefsful, to that of the well-grounded and fuccefsful ones.

The career of art, the great road which receives the footfteps of projeɕtors, may be confidered as a vaft, and perhaps unbounded, plain, beftrewed with gulphs, fuch as Curtius was fwallowed

L 2　　　　　up

up in. Each requires an human vic-
tim to fall into it ere it can close, but
when it once closes, it closes to open no
more, and so much of the path is safe
to those who follow. To tie men neck
and heels, and throw them into the gulphs
I have been speaking of, is altogether
out of the question : but if at every
gulph a Curtius stands mounted and ca-
parisoned, ready to take the leap, is it
for the legislator, in a fit of old woma-
nish tenderness, to pull him away?
Laying even public interest out of the
question, and considering nothing but
the feelings of individuals, a legislator
would scarcely do so, who knew the value of hope, " the most precious gift
" of heaven."

Consider

Confider, Sir, that it is not with the invention-lottery (that great branch of the project-lottery, for the fake of which I am defending the whole, and muft continue fo to do until you or fomebody elfe can fhew me how to defend it on better terms), it is not I fay with the invention-lottery, as with the mine-lottery, the privateering-lottery, and fo many other lotteries, which you fpeak of, and in no inftance I think, very much to their advantage. In thefe lines fuccefs does not, as in this, arife out of the embers of ill fuccefs, and thence propagate itfelf, by a happy contagion, perhaps to all eternity. Let Titius have found a mine, it is not the more eafy, but by fo much the lefs eafy, for Sem-

pronius

pronius to find one too : Let Titius have
made a capture, it is not the more eafy
but by fo much the lefs eafy, for Sem-
pronius to do the like. But let Titius
have found out a new dye, more bril-
liant or more durable than thofe in ufe,
let him have invented a new and more
convenient machine, or a new and more
profitable mode of hufbandry, a thoufand dyers, ten thoufand mechanics, a
hundred thoufand hufbandmen, may repeat and multiply his fuccefs : and then,
what is it to the public, though the fortune of Titius, or of his ufurer, fhould
have funk under the experiment ?

Birmingham and Sheffield are pitched
upon by you as examples, the one of a
pro-

projecting town, the other of an unpro-
jecting one * Can you forgive my faying, I rather wonder that this comparifon of your own choofing, did not fuggeft fome fufpicions of the juftice of the
conceptions you had taken up, to the
difadvantage of projectors. Sheffield is
an old oak : Birmingham, but a mufhroom. What if we fhould find the
mufhroom ftill vafter and more vigorous
than the oak ? Not but the one as well
as the other, at what time foever planted, muft equally have been planted by
projectors: for though Tubal Cain himfelf were to be brought poft from Arme-
nia to England to plant Sheffield, Tubal
Cain himfelf was as arrant a projector

* B. I. ch. x. vol. i. p. 176, edit. 8vo. 1784.

in

in his day, as ever Sir Thomas Lombe
was, or bifhop Blaife : but Birmingham, it feems, claims in common par-
lance the title of a projecting town, to
the exclufion of the other, becaufe, being
but of yefterday, the fpirit of project
fmells frefher and ftronger there than
elfewhere.

When the odious found of the word
projector no longer tingles in your ears,
the race of men thus ftigmatized do not
always find you their enemy. Projects,
even under the name of " dangerous
" and expenfive experiments," are re-
prefented as not unfit to be encouraged,
even though monopoly be the means :
and the monopoly is defended in that
inftance, by its fimilarity to other inftances,

ftances, in which the like means are employed to the like purpofe.

" When a company of merchants un-
" dertake at their own rifk and expence
" to eftablifh a new trade, with fome
" remote and barbarous nation, it may
" not be unreafonable" (you obferve)
" to incorporate them into a joint ftock
" company, and to grant them, in cafe
" of their fuccefs, a monopoly of the
" trade for a certain number of years.
" It is the eafieft and moft natural way,
" in which the ftate can recompenfe
" them, for hazarding a dangerous and
" expenfive experiment, of which the
" public is afterwards to reap the bene-
" fit. A temporary monopoly of this
                                    " kind

" kind may be vindicated, upon the
" fame principles, upon which a like
" monopoly of a new machine is granted
" to its inventor, and that of a new
" book to its author."

I have fometimes been tempted to
think that were it in the power of laws to
put *words* under profcription, as it is to
put *men*, the caufe of inventive induftry
might perhaps derive fcarcely lefs affiftance from a bill of attainder againft the
words *project* and *projectors*, than it has
derived from the act authorizing the
grant of patents. I fhould add, however, for a time : for even then the envy, and vanity, and wounded pride,
of the uningenious herd, would fooner
or later infufe their venom into fome
other

other word, and fet it up as a new tyrant, to hover, like its predeceffor, over
the birth of infant genius, and crufh it
in its cradle.

You have defended againft unme-
rited obloquy two claffes of men, the
one innocent at leaft, the other highly
ufeful; the fpreaders of Englifh arts in
foreign climes*, and thofe whofe induftry exerts itfelf in diftributing that neceffary commodity, which is called by
the way of eminence the ftaff of life.
May I flatter myfelf with having fucceeded at laft in my endeavours, to re-
commend to the fame powerful protec-

*B. IV. ch. 8. vol. ii. p. 514. *et alibi*, edit. 8vo.
1784.

tion,

tion, two other highly useful and equally
persecuted sets of men, usurers and projectors.—Yes—I will, for the moment
at least, indulge so flattering an idea :
and, in pursuance of it, leaving usurers, for whom I have said enough already, I will consider myself as joined
now with you in the same commission,
and thinking with you of the best means
of relieving the projector from the load
of discouragement laid on him by these
laws, in so far as the pressure of them
falls particularly upon him.   In my
own view of the matter, indeed, no
temperament, no middle course, is either necessary or proper : the only perfectly effectual, is the only perfectly
proper remedy,—a spunge. But, as
                              nothing

nothing is more common with mankind,
than to give oppofite receptions, to con-
clufions flowing with equal neceffity
from the fame principle, let us accom-
modate our views to that contingency.

According to this idea, the object,
as far as confined to the prefent cafe,
fhould be, to provide, in favour of projectors only, a difpenfation from the rigour of the anti-ufurious laws : fuch,
for inftance, as is enjoyed by perfons
engaged in the carrying trade, in virtue of the indulgence given to loans
made on the footing of *refpondentia* or
bottomry. As to abufe, I fee not why
the danger of it fhould be greater in
this cafe than in thofe. Whether a
fum

ſum of money be embarked, or not embarked, in ſuch or ſuch a new manu-
facture on land, ſhould not, in its own
nature, be a fact much more difficult
to aſcertain, than whether it be embarked, or not embarked, in ſuch or
ſuch a trading adventure by ſea : and,
in the one caſe as in the other, the payment of the intereſt, as well as the re-
payment of the principal, might be
made to depend upon the ſucceſs of the
adventure.

If the leading-ſtring is not yet thought
tight enough, boards of controul might
be inſtituted to draw it tighter.   Then
opens a ſcene of vexation and intrigue :
waſte of time conſumed in courting the
favour

favour of the members of the
board : wafte of time, in open-
ing their underftandings, clenched perhaps by ignorance, at any rate by dif-
dain and felf-fufficiency, and vanity,
and pride : the favour (for pride will
make it a favour) granted to fkill in the
arts of felf recommendation and cabal,
devoid of inventive merit, and refufed
to naked merit unadorned by practice
in thofe arts : wafte of time on the part
of the perfons themfelves engaged in
this impertinent inquiry : wafte of
fomebody's money in paying them for
this wafte of time. All thefe may be
neceffary evils, where the money to be
beftowed is public money : how idle
where it is the party's own ! I will not
                                      plague

plague you, nor myfelf, with enquiring
of whom fhall be compofed this board
of nurfes to grown gentlemen : were it
only to cut the matter fhort, one might
name at once the Committees of the So-
ciety of Arts. There you have a body
of men ready trained in the conduct of
enquiries, which refemble that in queftion, in every circumftance, but that
which renders it ridiculous : the members or reprefentatives of this democratic
body would be as likely, I take it, to
difcharge fuch a truft with fidelity and
fkill, as any ariftocracy that could be
fubftituted in their room.

Crichoff,
in White Ruffia,
March 1787.

F I N I S.

For EU product safety concerns, contact us at Calle de José Abascal, 56–1°,
28003 Madrid, Spain or eugpsr@cambridge.org.